STREAKS OF LIGHT

A practical manual
for opening your life
to God's light
through the Bible

Suddenly a light flashed
from the sky all around him.
(Acts 9:3, NEB)

Overton Sacksteder

Distributed by:
LOGOS INTERNATIONAL
Plainfield, NJ 07060

All Scripture references are taken from the King James Version (KJV), the New English Bible (NEB), and the Proposed Book of Common Prayer (PBCP).

STREAKS OF LIGHT
Copyright © 1980 by Overton Sacksteder
All rights reserved
Printed in the United States of America
Library of Congress Catalog Card Number: 79-92952
International Standard Book Number: 0-88270-420-6
Published by PBP, division of Logos International
Plainfield, New Jersey 07060

To the family of God at St. Michael and All Angels Church, Evansville, Indiana, without whose intercessions the miracle that spared my life and enabled me to publish this book might not have occurred.

Acknowledgment

Please Read This!

When an author begins with "I want to thank . . . ," people frequently stop reading, because they do not want to clutter their minds with faceless names. But often these acknowledgments give some clues about the author's makeup and this may well help the reader. I always read such acknowledgments to the last period and profit thereby. Therefore, I want to thank the following: St. Paul's Church, Jeffersonville, Indiana, who gave me an extra month off to start this book; Martha Hooper, who made the first draft coherent; Dr. David Humphrey and his wife, Carol, who struggled to make sense of this book as it tumbled out of my head; Dorothy Lewis, for her careful reading and shrewd criticism; Judy Manteufel, whose withering scorn purged the book of its grosser sexisms; and Robert Jenkins for the initial Xeroxing. At this point about eighty learners scattered in classes throughout Indiana wrestled with the first version, and their discussions revealed where the book was clear and where it was not. Then Fr. Brian Hall's shrewd suggestions on restructuring and his willingness to provide his secretary's help brought this version into being.

Certainly, high thanks are due to those persons around the country who spent well over 5,000 hours being counseled by me in the last twenty-five years, sharing their "streaks of light" with me as we struggled to make sense of a world that sometimes seemed senseless. Above all, thanks to my persuasive wife, Mary, who believed in this work when I had ceased to believe in it, and who made long and persistent pleas on its behalf. Finally, I want to express gratitude for the endless series of "streaks of light," a few of which are finitely transmitted herein, gratia Deo.

Foreword

The Purpose of This Book

This book is written out of my experience that the Bible is the basic tool for building a way of life wherein communication with God is a day-to-day reality. It provides a way to God for the common man. Yet, for a variety of reasons, the Bible has become inaccessible to the men and women in the pew. They long for more than the week-to-week contact with God afforded by worship in the Church, but are unable to find this through the Bible because they do not bring to its reading what was present in those who were God's instruments in producing it; namely, that God is the present and principal force in all mankind's history, collective and personal. The faith that He was there in His winsome and persuasive love enabled those who produced the Bible to discern His presence and to share it with us. In order for us to participate in this sharing we must bring to our meditations on Scripture our own faith and expectancy that He does constantly communicate to us in our history, collective and personal. Through an intuitive power in us, His Spirit provides the *Streaks of Light* which are His response to this faith and expectation.

A Word About Method

Each chapter reveals a different situation in which

this communication takes place. The title page for these will summarize what is to follow, forming a transition from the previous chapter to the next one and giving some notion of the new concepts to be introduced. These serve to tie the book together and to provide a framework for its development.

At the end of each chapter will be a short Discussion Guide consisting of two parts. The first will present two or three questions or topics for discussion based on the argument of the text itself. Then will follow a passage of Scripture not quoted in the chapter but illustrating the principles covered. Two categories of questions will follow:

1. Questions which deal generally with what God is telling us in the passage quoted.
2. Questions dealing generally with the way we have responded to what He has told us as we have lived our lives to this point.

Since no one is perfect, there will be a discrepancy between these two poles. If we are to live as God has made this world to be lived in we must resolve the differences in these two positions. The final topic for discussion is how this resolution might be brought about.

In order to make this method of discussion and study clearer, I have added an answer sheet to the first list of discussion questions. This should establish the pattern of this type of Bible meditation. However, there will be no answer sheets for any of the subsequent discussion questions, because it is not important what Scripture says to me but what it says to you. However, through the years I have found this method to be most productive of the streaks of light which illumine our understanding.

Contents

Introduction xi
1 Desert Hebrew, the Good News,
   and Modern Man.. 1
2 God Speaks to Us Through the Bible............ 13
3 The First Revolution of Moses..................... 23
4 The Bible and Its Sources........................... 33
5 The Second Revolution of Moses 47
6 The Lion Has Roared 61
7 The Impertinence of Job 77
8 Everyman and the Fall................................ 91
9 Jew and Greek... 103
10 Three Days in the Temple.......................... 115
11 What a Stranger Taught Our Lord 125
12 Jesus, the Law and Grace.......................... 135
13 The Finger of God..................................... 147
14 Three Long Hours..................................... 159
15 Emmaus and Afterwards........................... 173
16 Peter the Preacher 187
17 Saint Paul and the Football Coach 203
18 A Glimpse into Heaven............................. 217
   Afterword 229

Introduction:
For the Person in the Pew

For more than half my life I was able to isolate the Bible completely from me. Not that I had much to do with it. Everything connected with what passed for religious education conspired to put the Scriptures in the same category with hoop skirts and celluloid collars, objects of little interest and relevance today. Moreover, the Bible had about it an "aura of untouchableness." It was like the Constitution of the United States: almost everyone will eagerly swear to defend it, but hardly anyone will attempt to read and understand it. So formidable were these preconceptions of mine that I was able to reach a point of acceptance of the Christian faith which led me into the ministry with the Bible virtually untouched.

On one occasion in my early adolescence, my mother almost opened the door for me, albeit unwittingly. She told me of a time in her childhood when she was beset by a short-lived period of extreme dutiful piety and read the Bible daily. At this time her grandmother, who was in her last illness, called my mother to her side and solemnly asked, "Do you read your Bible every day?"

"Yes ma'am," said the girl proudly.

"Well don't," growled the old lady. "It's full of dirty old men."

Now this appealed to me. At that time I was seriously

contemplating a career as a dirty young man and no source seemed too unlikely to explore a few pointers. But, alas, I did not know where to look and this was not the sort of thing I was ready to ask mother. So I thrashed about in the early chapters of Genesis in search of something racy. What an exercise in futility! I came nowhere near the chapters on the destruction of Sodom and Gomorrah, and would not have understood them if I had.

I think more needs to be said about the aura of untouchableness that surrounds the Bible than just a passing reference, for I find that I am certainly not the only one to grow up with this impression. With many, it takes the form of seeing the Holy Bible as a kind of talisman, a good luck charm for a soldier to wear in his breast pocket to stop a bullet; or for the homemaker to put on the coffee table, as a kind of household god, to be dusted from time to time. Or others will hold its contents to be sacrosanct, maintaining that God speaking to Abraham or Moses belongs to a special age when it was God's habit to speak to men, a habit He has long since broken. These will look with hostility on any hint that God speaks to men today treating this as a kind of blasphemy, an attack on the Holy Book. Sometimes fundamentalists may be guilty of this, conceding that God may somehow make His thoughts known to men in their hearts, but things are not as they were with Abraham and Moses, when God spoke out loud. Perhaps we might concede that difference, if only to mention that the difference is not with God, who changes not, but with men, who change in the way they look at Him.

You may have guessed by now, that if for the first half of my life I was able to isolate myself from the Bible, during the latter part it got to me. You can also see that I believe that God continues to communicate with man as He always has and always will, not withstanding man's problems with loud and clear reception. The Bible exists, then, as a unique kind of textbook in the language God speaks when He communicates with us, and we are going to have to master this language to hear Him. I was very pleased with this analogy until I read it over. Now I see that it does not express my meaning as precisely as I had hoped. Understanding what God is communicating to you is not so much like learning a special language as it is mastering a way of thinking that opens your mind to what God is saying. I shall try to describe this way of thinking in such a manner that even if you don't accept it, you can at least recognize and understand it. This may also help you toward a sympathetic relationship with those who do accept it.

When it occurred to me to write this book, I went to my library shelves and took out all the books designed to make the Bible relevant. Then I made a stack of them on my desk top and measured it. Fifteen and one-half inches of books to make the Bible speak to the person in the pew! Suppose I had all that had been published on this subject in the past ten years. How tall would the stack be? Fifteen and one-half feet—fifteen and one-half miles, maybe! And then I said to myself, "Now, you idiot, who do you think you are and what do you think you're doing, adding yet another book to this pile?"

I must admit this cooled me off for a while. I slowly began to thumb through one of the books, looking at the table of contents, reading here and there, then picking up another, refreshing my memory about what it said until at last I arrived at a conclusion. All of these authors know much more about the Bible than I do. They know it as scholars, careful never to mix "ingesis" and "exegesis," always printing the original word in Hebrew or Greek, giving us all manner of the fruits from philological and archeological research, of textual criticism and form criticism, attempting to make the Bible relevant by surrounding it with a superabundance of knowledge.

This is not the way I know the Bible. I know it as a navigator knows his tables and charts as they relate to the stars of the heavens. It tells me where I have been and where I am going. Lest someone believe that I am saying that I know the Bible as a moral and ethical guide for my behavior, I must draw his attention to the analogy I have used and he will find that it is this and much more. Rather, the stars of heaven represent to the navigator a part of what God means to him, a reality to be understood in order to have a basis on which to set a course. The navigator consults his tables, decides which stars to observe, finds their location, makes his observation, returns to his tables, calculates and plots his position, and alters his course according to his actual location. While knowing God through Scripture is not quite as neat and easy for the believer as celestial navigation is for the mariner, there are many points of close similarity.

Familiarity with the stars and planets comes from a kind of interplay between observation and identification of what has been seen on star maps, finders, and, in the case of planets, the tables. However, while we rely on what is visual or mechanical in observing the heavens, we perceive God by relying on a wordless voice picked up by an inner ear. There is a difference in precision, certainly, although that split second when the star image exactly meets the horizon in the sextant, or the sun hangs at the top of its course before starting down at a noon sight, that instant when you intuit to shout "mark!" so that the time may be recorded, is very like the streak of light that flashes upon an inward eye during which God reveals to you one of His hidden truths.

You will note that I speak in terms of sensory images, a wordless voice picked up by an inner ear, light that flashes upon an inward eye. Yet it is not like this. Perhaps intuition does describe it better: that impulse of insight that suddenly clarifies the obscure, and causes us to say, "Oh, I see," when there is no visual image at all. Whatever this miraculous organ, however elusive to description, through which man senses intuitively, it exists as surely as breath itself in any man who can comprehend the meaning of these words. It is to this familiar if undefined organ that God addresses himself. He speaks to us constantly. Just as the stars are always overhead, He is always there with communication for us.

To many, the heavens are billions of tiny points of light in a black sky. To some, these larger pin points have names: Aldebaren, Sirius, Procyon, Betelgeuse, Canopus, Spica, Polaris. Moreover, their relationship to the earth in a moment of time can tell us where we are with an exactness that is only limited by our capacities of observation. Likewise, to many, this intuitive sense picks up an endless stream of inner chatter, undifferentiated, unidentified, and unheeded. To some, it is cultivated and understood, dimly; identified as divine insight, hopefully; perceived by a most imperfect instrument, admittedly. The intuitive sense needs to be diligently compared with Scripture and tested by the horse sense of the holy common people of God.

The point of all this is that the scholar, however much we admire and need him, however grateful we are to him for opening the Scriptures to us (and he has certainly done that for the clergy), is not the one to write the book on making the Bible relevant to the person in the pew. He knows too much of the wrong kind of thing. The scholar is compelled by the demands of his discipline to be absolutely accurate in verifying what he writes. His theories, when he expresses them, must conform to the data available.

I am under no such restriction since I am writing on the theory that what I don't know won't hurt you. The only scholarship I am concerned with is that which will help me deal with my readers' hang-ups. I know; I have been there. Fourteen years of my adult life were spent, partly with great reluctance and resistance, as a person in the pew. I remember my frustrations in trying conscientiously to deal with Scripture as something separate from and unrelated to my life: the futile search for an easy codified series of directions for living; my conviction that God's revelation to men was something complete and ended long ago; my unwillingness to accept a fundamentalist approach to the Bible; and my equal reluctance to accept it as merely good literature. So, when, as my brother put it, I became a professional hairsplitter, I determined to remember these things.

But times change and so do hang-ups. The things that bothered me have been sucked into the vortex of change and lost among a host of matters of graver consequence. I cannot write the same book I would like to have read twenty years ago. Nor can I write one that deals with the problems of the person in the pew today. These problems will change next week. Indeed, there is no collective "person in the pew"—only individual men and women, some still struggling with issues of 1890 and some trying to anticipate those of 1990.

Some believe the Church is inert and insensitive to the social issues of its time and some believe that she is so preoccupied with them that the gospel is neglected. Some seek the help of the Church in dealing with their domestic inquietudes and some would resent the interference of the Church into what they consider to be essentially private matters. Some make an idol of the institution and some call it the Antichrist. Who is the "person in the pew" that a book can be addressed to him or to her? If one is determined, as I am, to add another three-quarters of an inch to that formidable pile of books designed to make the Bible relevant to laymen, I must say more than, "I am writing for the person in the pew whom I understand as scholars do not," because this person doesn't exist with a single, unified set of needs, problems, or hang-ups.

But there is certainly one thing these men and women all have in common. They all have that intuitive sense; they all possess that miraculous organ through which God communicates. Some may be unaware that God communicates with them. Some may sense this only on rare occasions and some may be far more perceptive than I. It is my hope that this book may be useful to all—for some a means of discovery, and for others the confirmation and interpretation of what has already been experienced.

I am going to talk about some of the insights, these streaks of light which have illuminated some subjects that had been hitherto shrouded in darkness for me. Most of them are centered upon Scripture, although I don't intend to limit myself to the purely biblical. I consider the ultimate source of these concepts to be God, the Holy Spirit, and I hope that, despite the distortion, straining, pummeling, rending, stretching, and pulling they undergo as they pass through my mind, that the Spirit in you may recognize this source.

1

Desert Hebrew, the Good News, and Modern Man

In this chapter we move almost halfway around the world and nearly three thousand years backwards in time and enter into the world view of desert Hebrew where man listens to the voice of God and obeys. We contrast his way of thinking with our own and discover how God was accessible to him in a way He is hidden from us. We note how faithfully he preserves God's revelation to him even before he had a written language to transmit it. Abraham is compared and contrasted with a twentieth-century counterpart in the way they might deal with a similar situation. Finally, we show that the intuitive sense of God in our lives, tested by Scripture and shared in the praying community, develops our sensitivity to and eagerness for what God has to tell us.

The environment of a person forms the mode of his thought and the content of his vocabulary. It is some years since Neil Armstrong and Buzz Aldrin completed their walk, or should I say, their dance, on the moon, rejoined Mike Collins in Columbia, left orbiting the moon, and streaked toward earth. How many words and phrases have entered our vocabulary since Shorty Powers first described Alan Shepard's condition as "A-OK" in an early space flight? From "liftoff" and before to "splashdown" and after, phrases have entered our language which will remain to shape our thought for centuries. One day my brother-in-law, trusting soul, left me three and a half pounds of prime sirloin to broil. I asked him when he wanted to eat so I would know when to start the charcoal. He told me that he planned "ignition at five and liftoff at six." So there you are, perfectly clear communication and quite economical as a result of our space age environment. Twenty years ago this would have been incomprehensible.

With this phenomenon in mind let us consider the life and surroundings of the nomadic Hebrew roaming the desert in the second millennium before Christ, for it is his language and even more importantly, his mode of thought that is the basis of the religion the western world at least nominally espouses. What was his life like? Certainly it was very close to the basic unrefined elements of nature: the burning heat of the day and the bitter cold of the night, the harsh desert winds, the turbulent storms, the predatory wild beasts, the live volcano.

It was from these inhospitable elements of the earth that the Hebrew wrested a reluctant living, aware constantly of a power greater than his own. Because his concerns were centered on these basic life and death matters, his vocabulary was built on the words and concepts of survival. He had little time for daydreaming or speculation because of the constant imminence of danger. The frequency with which disaster struck and its violent force were constant reminders of man's own impotence. And yet, he usually survived.

It was in this survival that he began to sense that he was being protected. His reaction was one of gratitude. His response was one of worship. Certainly the Hebrew is not unique among men because he lived a hard life, sensed a provident God and gave in return his grateful worship. This pattern has been repeated over and over again in human history and the religions of the world spring from such origins. But perhaps out of untold centuries of lonely, dangerous nomadic existence there developed among the Hebrews an unusual sensitivity to God's way with men. Perhaps the unrelenting poverty and austerity of his situation increased his diligence in seeking to know God's mind for him and made him more realistic in discerning it. However it happened, these little Hebrew tribes saw God behind everything great or trivial that crossed their paths or their minds. Much later Israel gave this mind-set expression in one of his songs, but the reality predates by many centuries this expression of it.

Where could I go to escape your spirit?
Where could I flee from your presence?
If I climb the heavens, you are there,
there too, if I lie in Sheol.
(Ps. 139:7-8 PBCP)

So if the Hebrew had God on his mind and in his heart, he also had Him on his lips and in his songs. He spoke of God and sang of God with the words he knew: the words of earth, sky, sheep, men, and nature as he knew them. He called his God a *living* God, just as he called the wolf or the lion that attacked his sheep a living animal. This contrasted to the sheep themselves which were not living but domesticated animals. God, like the lion, was untamed. He could not be bent to man's will but man must bend to His. He was unlike the domesticated gods of the fertility cults that could be placated and made to do the will of men. All this meaning is implied in the term *living God* which falls so easily on twentieth-century ears and evokes so little. So whenever the Hebrew speaks of a quality in God, he borrows a term from the life he leads because he knows no other words to use. His language does not provide him abstract terms for the niceties of theological discussion. Particularly in its primitive stage his was a concrete language. God is described as inhabiting the body of a man because there is no other manner of describing Him that assures his existence.

Let me clarify this. The Hebrew believes that anything that was good that entered his mind came there because God sent it. He sent it by way of one of His messengers who appear in English translations of the Bible as angels. To us "angel" is a highly specialized theological term and evokes all sorts of images of halos, wings, and white nightgowns. Not so with the Hebrew. The term is as unspecialized as our word messenger and means much the same thing. The Hebrew lacked inclination, if not vocabulary, to say, "I have an idea." Rather, he would say, "The Angel of the Lord came unto me and he said. . ." by which he meant the same thing. Yet, because when we are inspired, our inward sight is not assaulted with huge wings and white robes, we are likely to think that God has changed His way of doing things, and no longer sends His angels to men.

Even more commonly, the Lord simply spoke in the mind of the hearer:

> The Lord said to Abram, 'Leave your own country, your kinsmen, and your father's house, and go to a country that I will show you. I will make you into a great nation, I will bless you and make your name so great that it shall be used in blessings:
>> Those that bless you I will bless,
>> those that curse you, I will execrate.
>> All the families on earth
>> will pray to be blessed as you are blessed.'
>
> (Gen. 12:1-3 NEB)

It is improbable that this represents a verbatim reproduction of a conversation between Abraham and God. While the accounts of the patriarchs are generally considered to be tribal rather than personal memories, a good case can be made for the historical existence of Abraham about 1800 B.C. Since the earliest manuscripts of the Old Testament date from about the tenth century B.C. it is highly unlikely that a detailed conversation would be remembered for eight or nine hundred years just as it was held. Not that I am knocking oral tradition; the Hebrews maintained a chain of such tradition with tremendous integrity which has preserved for us in essence, if not in actual detail, what happened to them before they began to write their history down. Young boys, especially chosen for the purpose, began learning the history of the tribe very early and recited it all their lives, teaching it in turn to other youngsters coming up. Moreover, where there is no writing, memory is much more reliable than in cultures where things can be written down.

We have one cultural phenomenon that can give us some notion of how oral tradition works: the transmission of a joke. You can, we'll say, be present at the original telling of a joke in New York and a week later you can hear the same story, its essence accurately preserved, in San Francisco. Or, you may hear a joke you heard twenty years ago, substantially unchanged. There may be two or three variations which crop up, and the embellishment will reflect the creativity of the many tellers who have made their individual contributions, but the plot remains recognizable. Because of our lack of interest in and skill to maintain an accurate oral tradition in the telling of stories, variations and changes will occur in a relatively short time, changes which would have taken centuries to take place in the oral tradition of the Hebrew tribes.

With all this in mind, let us turn and reread the passage from Genesis quoted above. It is impossible to reconstruct what actually happened in history that forms the basis of the passage. But it does tell us with great precision how the Hebrews looked upon the way God called them to be His people. It was very easy for them to accept this as a conversation between God and Abraham because it reflected the way the Hebrews thought and had thought for centuries, and they were certain that this accurately represented the way Abraham's mind would have worked.

Let me illustrate by making a contrast. An executive in middle management in an American industry is called by his company to take an extremely important and well-paid position in a distant city. To accept this would assure his future and enable him to provide for his family more lavishly than he could otherwise have done. True, it may remove him far from his own or his wife's family, and it uproots his children from their friends, but the promises of prosperity override all this and he decides to go. Now, it does not occur to him that God is calling him to make this move, or at least that he should consider this in the light of God's will for him. He simply does not think in these terms. It is as if Abraham thought in this way: "I have heard of a land with plenty of room, a land called Canaan, flowing with milk and honey. I know that if I leave I must leave my family and kindred, but in such a situation I can afford to raise a large family and have room for many descendants to live in prosperity."

Similar matter is being thought through in both cases. In one, the source of the matter is identified ultimately as God, because He is the source of everything. In the other, the matter is identified as circumstances or opportunity about which a decision must be made. I suppose that here is the crux of the

God is dead argument, for in the biblical revelation, God is the instigator of the action while in the contemporary situation He seems to have no part in it.

It is my contention that Abraham, by recognizing God calling him to move, was able to discern the intent of God in issuing the promises: "All the families on earth will pray to be blessed as you are blessed." By leaving God out of his consideration, the deciding factor in the decision of the executive is economic. If he were attuned to the voice of God, he would be sensitive to God's intent in issuing the call. He would know, first of all, whether the demands of the new position agreed with his abilities and talents. He would ask himself whether it is in harmony with what he considers to be his Christian vocation. Further, he would be concerned about the ethical and moral demands of the new situation. Do they square with the code he lives by? Finally, is the service he is called to render compatible with his understanding of God's will for the world? Are the goods and services provided by this operation meaningful and important to mankind? These are considerations which will produce satisfaction and fulfillment in the work situation, rather than the money, which, while important, should not be the sole determining factor. When one is sensitive to God's voice within, a promotion, such as the one described above, is seen in terms of whatever understanding of God's purpose the executive may have had.

How is this understanding of God's purpose for one developed? It is the task of a lifetime, one which is never completely or perfectly finished on this earth. And the ability to hear God's voice through the intuitive sense, while absolutely necessary, cannot be the sole factor in understanding God's purpose for our lives. To follow one's own inner sense exclusively without any frame of reference is to flirt with fanaticism or just plain nuttiness in religion. A parable will illustrate.

There was once a minister who had a sensitive face with deep, soulful eyes. His hands with their long, tapering fingers were beautifully expressive. He was much in demand to conduct quiet days for women's groups in various churches because he did so with such deep spirituality. His was a "spiritual" ministry indeed.

The content of his meditations developed mostly from poems he had written or from his own thought. He had little to do with his brother clergy and we felt that perhaps he found us a little coarse grained and earthy for him, with our occasional interest in the Dodgers or the Green Bay Packers.

At clergy conferences he would keep to himself, walking alone in the woods, a faraway look in his eyes, while the rest of us engaged in various kinds of shop talk, or went on about our favorite sports hero. There came a time of crisis in this man's life, but he did not seek counsel or advice from his brother clergy, nor did he search Scriptures for guidance. He closeted himself for the nine days of prayer and fasting; then he divorced his wife and married his organist. Now any one of us could have told him that if this was what he wanted to do, to go ahead and do it, but that he shouldn't pretend that in so doing he was doing the will of God. We have all met this person in one situation or another, this person who says, "I am a righteous person; therefore, whatever I want to do is righteous." While they may appeal to prayer or, in some cases, Scripture to support such action, what they do lacks the authenticity of what is divinely inspired.

While the intuitive sense is indispensable, there are two other major frames of reference which serve to keep us on the track. One of these is the Bible itself, not the Bible of the proof text or the fundamentalist interpretation, but the set of mind behind the Bible and everywhere manifested in it, which can give us a check for the authenticity of our intuitive sense. The other is in the praying community, wherein the insights one receives must be tested and shared. Perhaps this is most simply and conveniently done through a spiritual guide. My own opinion is that such a guide is extremely necessary, if not indispensable for this normalizing process. But in addition to that, there should be a sharing of insights and understanding within the community itself. This combination of God, the Holy Spirit, speaking to us in our hearts, as well as through the Church when cultivated carefully and diligently, furnishes the means by which He reveals to us the meaning of our creation, the purpose of our existence and our ultimate destiny.

So the sound of a wordless voice on the inner ear, streaks of light that flash across the inward eye, desert Hebrew translated beautifully but now somewhat incomprehensibly into King James's English and our own contemporary dialogue in the vernacular with other Christians—these are the media through which God speaks to us. It is the intercommunication and interaction among all three that enable us to grow in our understanding of, our sensitivity to, and our eagerness for what God has to tell us.

Discussion Guide

This guide is meant for use by a single reader discussing what he had read with his alter ego, or a group who may be studying this book together and want to pool their insights. It is a time to consider what has been said and to test the content so far to see if it evokes a response in you.

Try to put yourself into the skin of Abraham (Abram). Can you see why he was open to God because he expected God to speak to him? Shut your eyes and see if you can find that openness in yourself. Remember too, that Abraham's experience of God often took the form of discerning divine action and judgment in his own personal history. The passage below will illustrate.

> Abram's wife Sarai had borne him no children. Now she had an Egyptian slave-girl whose name was Hagar, and she said to Abram, 'You see that the Lord has not allowed me to bear a child. Take my slave-girl; perhaps I shall found a family through her.' Abram agreed to what his wife said; so Sarai, Abram's wife, brought her slave-girl, Hagar the Egyptian, and gave her to her husband Abram as a wife. When this happened Abram had been in Canaan for ten years. He lay with Hagar and she conceived; and when she knew that she was with child, she despised her mistress. Sarai said to Abram, 'I have been wronged and you must answer for it. It was I who gave my slave-girl into your arms, but since she has known that she is with child, she has despised me. May the Lord see justice done between you and me.' Abram replied to Sarai, 'Your slave-girl is in your hands; deal with her as you will.' So Sarai ill-treated her and she ran away.
>
> (Gen. 16:1-6 NEB)

Now God is saying something to Abram in this snippet of his personal history and it is something that by extension can be applied to each of us in perhaps a different way. What do you perceive Him saying to Abram? Scripture is rich in messages which each person can perceive in terms of his own life.

When you decide to meditate on a passage of Scripture, try to find out what God is saying to you.

What He says to me in the above passage goes something like this: "You have had my assurance over and over again, that if you do things my way, as unlikely as it may seem at the time, things will come out as I have promised. But when you lack faith in me as Sarai and Abram did, and take matters into your own hands, all concerned are miserable. See how misery spreads to the three in this instance. Hagar does not see that I, the Lord, made her conceive, but gives herself the glory and uses it as an excuse to be uppity and arrogant to her mistress. Sarai is hurt by this because it serves to reinforce in her the knowledge that I, the Lord, make women fertile or barren and that my promise was to her as well as Abram, and that her faithlessness has brought this arrogance upon her. Abram, too, knows that he has behaved faithlessly by taking Hagar to his bed, and as a result must see the mother of his first child mistreated until she runs into the desert to have his child alone."

Now each person has to apply this lesson to his life as it fits. I am sure that it takes only a little memory to dredge up some incident of our failure to accept and live by God's promise to us, and we can see the misery that failure spreads among all concerned. So the first thing we might ask when we read a passage is, "What is God saying to me?" You may want to write it down. It may be one thing. It may be five. Then we could ask, "What have I done about it?" We may have done all kinds of things about it. We may have been evasive, defensive, rebellious, faithless, or even obedient. You may also want to write this down, too. I like to write my meditations but my wife hates to. She says it quenches her spirit. Then ask yourself, "How can I resolve the discrepancy between what I do and what God wants me to do. This is called the resolution. It is not like a New Year's resolution, but a recognition of a course of action resolving the differences between God's way and ours. A resolution for Abraham in the above passage might go something like this. "When I decide what is impossible and take matters into my own hands, disaster and misery result. I have to believe that when God promises me (whatever way that communication may come) that He means it, and my only resolution of these difficulties is to trust Him." Read the next chapter and see the extent to which Abraham made such a resolution and the lengths he went to carry it out.

2

God Speaks to Us Through the Bible

In this chapter we speak of one of the most obvious examples of God's communication with man: Abraham's offering of his son, Isaac, to God. But we are not dealing with the obvious aspects of the event: Abraham's faithfulness in bringing the son of God's promise to be sacrificed; his strict though painful obedience to God's command; and God's providing the animal sacrifice in recognition of Abraham's faithfulness. But we are more concerned with how Abraham knew what the will of God was in the same way that we can know it in our lives. This is an attempt to relate the way God speaks to Abraham to the way He speaks to us. If we see this connection it will not only open the way that God speaks to us through the Bible, but also in our day to day lives.

Human Sacrifice and Father Abraham

The remarks in the previous chapter concerning oral tradition and verbal transmission in respect to Abraham apply equally to the passage below.

The time came when God put Abraham to the test. 'Abraham,' he called, and Abraham replied, 'Here I am.'

God said, 'Take your son Isaac, your only son, whom you love, and go to the land of Moriah. There you shall offer him as a sacrifice on one of the hills which I will show you.'

So Abraham rose early in the morning and saddled his ass, and he took with him two of his men and his son Isaac; and he split the firewood for the sacrifice, and set out for the place of which God had spoken.

On the third day Abraham looked up and saw the place in the distance.

He said to his men, 'Stay here with the ass while I and the boy go over there; and when we have worshipped we will come back to you.'

So Abraham took the wood for the sacrifice and laid it on his son Isaac's shoulder; he himself carried the fire and the knife, and the two of them went on together.

Isaac said to Abraham, 'Father,' and he answered, 'What is it, my son?' Isaac said, 'Here are the fire and the wood, but where is the young beast for the sacrifice?'

Abraham answered, 'God will provide himself with a young beast for a sacrifice, my son.' And the two of them went on together and came to the place of which God had spoken. There Abraham built an altar and arranged the wood. He bound his son Isaac and laid him on the altar on top of the wood.

Then he stretched out his hand and took the knife to kill his son; but the angel of the Lord called to him from heaven, 'Abraham, Abraham.' He answered, 'Here I am.'

The angel of the Lord said, 'Do not raise your hand against the boy; do not touch him. Now I know that you are a God-fearing man. You have not withheld from me your son, your only son.'

Abraham looked up, and there he saw a ram caught

by its horns in a thicket. So he went and took the ram and offered it as a sacrifice instead of his son.
(Gen. 22:1-13 NEB)

The kernel of historical fact behind the well-known story of Abraham and Isaac is, like the rest of the Abraham saga, almost impossible to recapture. Perhaps the event occurred something like this: The Hebrews were well aware that many of their neighbors and some of their ancestors practiced human sacrifice. This may have been the embellishment of a traditional narrative within their culture which told when and how human sacrifice was abandoned in favor of animal offerings. Perhaps, as the story was retold the episode was attributed to Abraham. This was a common device of the culture. For example, there are two accounts of the slaying of Goliath—the earlier one attributing it to an obscure warrior, Elhanan, while the latter, more glorious account made David the hero (1 Sam. 17). But to boggle over seeming discrepancies like this is to miss the real point of what is being told to us, and why.

Examine the biblical words with which God tested Abraham as they are recorded in verses one and two.
"Abraham!"
"Here I am."
"Take your son Isaac, your only son, whom you love, and go to the land of Moriah. There you shall offer him as a sacrifice on one of the hills which I will show you."

Now look at a paraphrase of these words in a form more familiar to us.
CONSCIENCE: "Abraham!"
ABRAHAM: "Okay, here I am."
CONSCIENCE: "That boy of yours is getting pretty big. He's almost past the age when he should

be taken and offered as a sacrifice in the custom of your forefathers."

ABRAHAM: "But he is my only son and I love him."

CONSCIENCE: "What difference can that make? Either you are obedient or you're not. Get on up the mountain with him and find a suitable place."

Whether the memory actually goes back to Abraham or not is really unimportant. What is much more relevant is, that if instead of the offering of the son in sacrifice, the issue had been to bring him to the bishop to be confirmed, or the equivalent, this dreary little drama would have a familiar ring. Yet the sacrifice story does present some difficulties.

For one thing, Genesis tells us that it was God who said these things to Abraham and our paraphrase imagines it to be the voice of conscience with the voice of God. What God says is infallible, indeed, the only infallibility that exists. What conscience says is the product of its content, and the content of conscience is conditioned by fallible, human social, and environmental factors. Yet the teaching of the Church has always been, in theory if not in practice, that the conscience must always be followed. But there is this corollary: the conscience must constantly be under instruction.

Look at it this way. Conscience is a capacity, given by God, through which we can know right from wrong. At birth it is an empty capacity, but as we grow it is filled with what we learn from parents, school, society, and our religion. Let us suppose that a youngster was reared in a somewhat nutty family who had the notion that baked beans came directly from Satan and even to taste them was to fall into grievous sin. All his life this young man has dutifully avoided baked beans in spite of frequent temptations—such as when they were the principal item on the school lunch menu—and the prospect of an afternoon of gnawing hunger pangs and the appetizing smell of the beans made the struggle difficult.

However, when he went to college and began expressing his freedom in other ways, he boldly ordered a serving of baked beans, and he suffered, guess what—a terrific attack of conscience! While the subject matter of this little illustration is ridiculous enough, the principle is not. Many pangs of conscience are produced in the young needlessly and foolishly, and guilts are developed that are sometimes sources of real psychological difficulty. Therefore, conscience cannot be considered an infallible guide to human behavior.

Yet, we are told that conscience must always be followed. What kind of double talk is this? One's conscience can be so wrong that following it would be damaging to the personality, yet one is always supposed to follow it.

Christianity is a religion of paradox and one definition of paradox is a contradiction with a resolution. When the conscience is troubled, instruction should be sought. It is quite possible that the conscience may be demonstrated to be in error, and the error can be conscientiously accepted. However, if the conscience is to grow and develop into a sensitive and reliable instrument, one should not always return to the person or group that instructed it in the first place. Since the Church is divided into sects, counsel may be sought from a denomination other than one's own in order to be freed from sectarian narrowness. For this reason, it is a great blessing that most of the work done on college campuses is ecumenical in character. This, theoretically, at least, makes available to the student a wider point of view at the time he is doing his greatest questioning of the values his conscience has accumulated.

After all this wind, the question still remains as to

whether the Hebrew friend who gave us this account of Abraham and Isaac was in error and confused the voice of Abraham's conscience with the voice of God, or whether I was wrong in suggesting that Abraham was listening to his conscience. It may be true that the voice of God and the voice of conscience are not to be confused; yet it is equally true that God, the Holy Spirit, may speak to us through our conscience, perhaps as our Hebrew friend suggests, if only to test us. We instinctively rebel at the notion that God is deliberately testing us, although in the Lord's Prayer we take the precaution of asking Him not to.

Since, in the mind of the Hebrew, everything good comes from God, how else will God be able to reveal to Abraham that animal sacrifice is a sufficient offering for him? He must first get Abraham up on the mountain and on the point of sacrificing Isaac, so that He can send His messenger to show him the meaning of a ram caught in a nearby bush. Therefore, I am willing to settle in my own mind for God's having used Abraham's conscience in order to prod him up the mountain in the first place. And in so doing, we can see that God's prodding of Abraham is certainly not unlike the way He prods us from time to time.

But let's return to what must have been an agonizing journey up the mountain. We notice that God mentions to Abraham that He will tell him of one of the mountains where he can make his burnt offering. Next we hear that Abraham, after making his preparations, sets out for the place of which God had told him. Then again, on the third day, he sees the place far off. As we read this, it appears that God has given specific and definite instructions to Abraham as to where to go. This, again, does not sound like anything we would experience. However, I am not so sure.

Have you ever lost something, hunted for it without

finding it, then, when you were about to give up, suddenly, as if by chance, your eyes went to a totally unlikely place and you found the lost object? This happens to me quite often with collar buttons. The round collar we Episcopalians wear has advantages which commend it and disadvantages that must be taken in stride. Yet, I have never really been able to make my peace with the collar button. These are hard to come by. Whenever I get a new supply, I very quickly lose all but the minimal two, and then begins the business of losing, searching, giving up; then, a random look and the find. My Hebrew friend would maintain that God shows me where the collar button is, and though it is hard for me to imagine the Almighty concerning himself with such trifles, either He is omniscient or He isn't. Further, I can't find any other reason why I should have cast my eye in some totally unlikely place and found there the missing article. Perhaps the angel of the Lord comes unto me, and says, "Look there!"

However, I do not believe that it was in this way that God told Abraham about the place where he should sacrifice. I believe God used Abraham's memory in telling him. It might have worked like this: around the house, I fancy myself as something of a handyman, and try to repair whatever I can. Many a time I have needed some odd bit of material and have remembered that I stuck a piece away five years ago that will just do the trick. This may be the first time in those five years I've thought about this one particular scrap, yet, in an unbelievable collection of junk, I go right to it, and find that it just fits.

Now, my Hebrew friend would have said that God told me where to find what I needed. In the same way he would say that God put into Abraham's mind the memory of a level shelf on the mountainside with many stones about for building an altar, and with a grove of trees with thick undergrowth beneath. If we accept his assumption that God and His providence are behind all things, how can we argue?

There is no way we can really improve the stark biblical account of what happened as Abraham and Isaac trudged up the mountain and made ready for the sacrifice. It is obvious that Isaac was not in on the proceedings until he found himself being bound and placed upon the wood. One wonders what trauma remained with him as a result of seeing his father, whom he loved and trusted, raise his knife against him, only to lower it again.

What really caused Abraham to put down the sacrificial instrument? We have ruled out beings with halos and wings, so we will have to say that God sent His messenger into Abraham's mind in the form of an idea, probably much like this: "Abraham, listen to me. You have come all this way and have demonstrated your faithfulness and obedience to God in your willingness to offer your only son. There is a noise in the bushes. At least lift up your eyes; look over at that thicket, and see what the disturbance is, for God has provided the lamb for the sacrifice as you said He would."

The subconscious awareness of the ram caught in the thicket sent the message or triggered the idea, whichever way you want to interpret it. At least Isaac and untold numbers of his descendants were saved from being sacrificed and the burnt offering of animals entered the religious practice of the Hebrew people.

At the risk of belaboring the point, I want to make it clear that, as I have tried to demonstrate, it is possible to translate God's voice from the biblical context into the way we think. I am not saying that God did not talk to Abraham, or reveal things to him, or that all the patriarch experienced is explainable in our modern modes of thought and expression. I am saying that God uses these modern modes to communicate with us, and we need to develop the mind-set that enables us to hear Him. As we read these accounts of God's revelation of himself to men in the Bible, and as we develop some skill and imagination in turning them into familiar thought processes, we should also begin to hear the voice of God speaking to us and become more and more sensitive to His providence and His all-embracing love.

Some will look upon this description of this relationship with God as most adolescent and dependent, but I can only say that these people have never tried to live in it. Nothing is more demanding of all that we have been given, including the opportunities, nothing offers greater freedom to be oneself than that which grows out of this kind of communication and relationship. If you don't believe it, see how Moses makes out in the next chapter.

Discussion Guide

We have seen the relationship between the way Abraham perceived God's will and the way we perceive it and I hope I have made my point. The difference is certainly not in the method used to communicate, but if a difference exists at all, it is a difference in the intensity of Abraham's expectation that God would communicate with him and ours that He will communicate with us. The more we expect God's communication to us, the more we perceive it. Here is a passage from the end of Abraham's life. He is speaking to his servant.

'I want you to swear by the Lord, the God of heaven and earth, that you will not take a wife for my son from the women of the Canaanites in whose land I dwell; you must go to my own country and to my own kindred to find a wife for my son Isaac.' The servant said to him, 'What if the woman is unwilling to come with me to this country? Must I in that event take your son back to the land from which you came?' Abraham said to him, 'On no account are you to take my son back there. The Lord the God of heaven who took me from my father's house and the land of my birth, the Lord who swore to me that he would give this land to my descendants—he will send his angel before you, and from there you shall take a wife for my son. If the woman is unwilling to come with you, then you will be released from your oath to me; but you must not take my son back there.'

(Gen. 24:3-8 NEB)

In this passage Abraham is assuring himself that he will do his part to see that God's promise to him will be kept. What does God communicate to Abraham that causes him to instruct his servant as he did? Does he leave a way open for God to act in his own terms in the event that the means Abraham has chosen does not work out? What does the passage say to us about the continuing implication of God's will for us? How have we responded to this? If you find a discrepancy between God's will and your way of carrying it out, how can you resolve it?

3

The First Revolution of Moses

Very few persons in the world's history have been endowed with a religious sensitivity and capacity for innovation in the man-to-God relationship that they can properly be called religious revolutionaries. Outstanding among these revolutionaries was Moses. Because of his intense relationship with the Almighty, he was able to see Him as the world's single unifying force, the ground of all being, and the fountainhead from which all else springs. This was indeed a revolution which has made God accessible to countless generations coming after in a unique new way. As you read this chapter, try to think like Moses, looking into the burning bush, feeling the aura of holiness about you and kicking off your shoes so you will not soil the holy ground on which you stand. Perhaps you can capture for yourself a bit of the experience of Moses.

Moses was steeped in the religion of what we can now properly call Israel. He was well acquainted with the lore of his people at this time when their faith was prominent in their thought. The Israelites, like most peoples, were more devout in adversity than in prosperity. It is certain that the bondage in Egypt heightened their devotion. How close Moses' contact was with Egypt and the Egyptians is a matter of conjecture, but it is obvious that he knew his own faith and knew it well.

When he fled Pharaoh's palace after killing the Egyptian, his solitude in the desert gave him a great deal of time for meditation at the very throne of God. God's "headquarters" for Israel were Mount Sinai, sometimes referred to as Mount Horeb, a live volcano in Moses' time. (At this time in history the God of Israel was the God of the storm and the God of the volcano.) Moses' relationship with his father-in-law, Jethro, who was a priest of Midian, no doubt furnished some of the content for his meditations. The Midianite beliefs were close to the religious traditions of Israel and, therefore, often furnished different versions of the same material with which Moses was familiar. The preoccupation with the faith of Israel and of Midian, the holy atmosphere of the mount, the solitude, all these circumstances turned the mind of Moses toward God in an extraordinary way and made him unusually sensitive to God's voice.

It was on just such a lonely occasion that Moses encountered God in the burning bush. The resulting insights altered his understanding of God to such an extent that it is not stretching things to call them the first of Moses' two religious revolutions. The account, as it comes down to us in the third chapter of Exodus, has had considerable embellishment in detail, but the heart of a genuine and profound meeting with the Almighty is preserved therein. In the first six verses of this chapter we meet some concepts already familiar to us.

Moses was minding the flock of his father-in-law Jethro, priest of Midian. He led the flock along the side of the wilderness and came to Horeb, the mountain of God.

There the angel of the Lord appeared to him in the

flame of a burning bush. Moses noticed that, although the bush was on fire, it was not being burnt up; so he said to himself, 'I must go across to see this wonderful sight.

Why does not the bush burn away?'

When the Lord saw that Moses had turned aside to look, he called to him out of the bush, 'Moses, Moses.' And Moses answered, 'Yes, I am here.'

God said, 'Come no nearer; take off your sandals; the place where you are standing is holy ground.'

Then he said, 'I am the God of your forefathers, the God of Abraham, the God of Isaac, the God of Jacob.' Moses covered his face, for he was afraid to gaze on God.

(Exod. 3:1-6 NEB)

The setting of this encounter is a grassy plain below Mount Sinai where Moses brought his flocks. We can imagine that he has climbed up a short distance onto the mountain for a better view of any approaching danger to his sheep; there he sees something that can be expected on an active volcano: a jet of flame seeming to come from the midst of a bush. Notice that first God sends His messenger to call Moses' attention to the phenomenon, or in our terms, the thought struck him that there was something extraordinary here that required closer scrutiny. As Moses investigated the unusual occurrence, he was filled with an overwhelming sense of God's presence. And as he stood there he began to perceive that the God of the storm, the God who resided in the volcano, was the God of his fathers.

Now to anyone who has a nodding acquaintance with Genesis and Exodus, it would seem obvious that this was believed from the time of Abraham himself.

Still we must remember that these books were subject to a great deal of editing from a monotheistic point of view. The various additions to the text make it seem that Israel was strongly monotheistic from the time it could be properly called Israel. Fortunately for us, these various editors habitually commented on the older material, but it seems they did not often change or delete any of it. When the older material is read, minus the editing, it becomes quite apparent that it is with Moses that characteristic monotheism has its beginning. This revelation of God to Moses in the burning bush was an innovation. If the idea of one God was so well accepted at Moses' time, why did God trouble himself to reveal it?

Almost as profound and far reaching is the revelation in the two verses quoted below.

Then Moses said to God, 'If I go to the Israelites and tell them that the God of their forefathers has sent me to them, and they ask me his name, what shall I say?'

God answered, 'I AM; that is who I am. Tell them that I AM has sent you to them.'
(Exod. 3:13-14 NEB)

Moses' need to know the name of God requires a little explanation. To us a name does not mean a great deal, but to the desert nomad it indicated tribe, kindred, and, most importantly, whether the person was friend or foe and could be trusted. So Moses required of God some means of proving to the people that he had indeed spoken to the Lord. The gods of the time all had their identifying lineage, and Moses probably expected something of the sort. As he meditated on the question, God opened his understanding. The revelation is indeed remarkable even if the exact Hebrew is obscure. While it is impossible to translate the Lord's reply precisely, the meaning is clear. The use of a form of the verb "to be" indicated that the name of God, to use Paul Tillich's fine paraphrase, is "the ground of being."

"Thus shalt thou say unto the children of Israel, I AM hath sent me to you." This is identification enough. Other gods may rise from the sea or be children of the sun and the earth, but the God who is the basis of all existence ends forever the necessity for interminable regressions. Moses knew the name of God and had the credentials he needed to return to his people and carry out the task God required of him. But still he dragged his feet. As much as I am tempted to talk about this now, I want to reserve the subject of Moses' call for a chapter devoted to the call of the prophets in general. Let's move on to the hardhearted Pharaoh.

My own feeling about the account of the plagues of Egypt is that they are memories of a composite of events telescoped into a smaller time than actually occurred. Most seem to have been natural phenomena. Read, for example these two verses.

> So Moses and Aaron did as the Lord had commanded. He lifted up his staff and struck the water of the Nile in the sight of Pharaoh and his courtiers, and all the water was changed into blood.
>
> The fish died and the river stank, and the Egyptians could not drink water from the Nile. There was blood everywhere in Egypt.
>
> (Exod. 7:20-21 NEB)

Then compare that account with this excerpt from an article in The Indianapolis Star dated August 3, 1969, describing the wholesale death of fish in Louisiana.

> Red tides are caused by microscopic red plants. When conditions are right . . . the salt organisms

bloom, giving off a poison deadly to fish. The plant is known to scientists as gymondinium brevis.

In the past it has been common for people to say, when they make a comparison like this, "Aha! It is just as I thought. You really can't believe the Bible after all. All these things that God is given credit for are purely natural happenings with rational scientific explanations. When will we abandon this anachronistic religious belief and begin to live in terms of the promise of this enlightened age?"

Indeed, we have been encountering this reasoning since the eighteenth century in one form or another. And though our religion has been judged anachronistic, outdated, and God has been pronounced dead, and several obituaries have been written, our faith continues to have an amazing vitality. I like to create little scenarios that sometimes express ideas better than straight prose, and I have one in mind to explain the failure of God to remain dead. This encounter will make some little demand on your imagination because it takes place between a very enlightened, though kindly product of our scientific and technological age and Moses. How they got together is not important. The product speaks.

"Moses, I know you believe that God, as you understand Him, intervened as you led the children of Israel through the water, and while I wouldn't want to do anything at all to destroy your faith, I do think, however, as an intelligent person you should examine some of the facts.

"First of all, the place where you crossed is a little marshy section called the Sea of Reeds, rather than the Red Sea itself. Second, the area is known for its extraordinary range of winds and tides. Undoubtedly you and your people crossed on an extremely low tide, and the following high tide and high winds inundated the forces of Pharaoh. So really, the whole crossing can be explained by natural causes."

"Certainly," replied Moses. "That is how God did it."

It made little difference to Moses whether God acted through nature or whether He set aside nature and acted in ways we consider miraculous, because in his mind, it was God acting. For Moses there were no accidents or coincidences. All resulted from the providence and concern of the Almighty.

It seems fashionable today to believe that this aspect of the Christian faith is somehow degrading to man, that it makes him a dependent creature and keeps him from realizing the best that is in him. However, if you have accepted by now that, in spite of the Hebraicisms through which the story is told, Moses searches the depths of himself and receives ideas and inspirations on how to proceed next, much as modern man receives them, then you realize that Moses is more rather than less of a man through his relationship with God. After first one thing then another, Pharaoh's heart is hardened and back comes Moses with yet another scheme to force Pharaoh to let his people go.

So it is with the scientist doggedly seeking a solution to a problem through research. One thing after another fails, and back he comes with this inspiration and that, until finally the problem is solved. My contention is that in both cases God is the revealer, the inspirer, and that in one case He is recognized and in the other He is not.

Sometimes I think that one of the real differences that the gift of the Holy Spirit makes in baptism comes from the consciousness that He has been given. The unbeliever has God dwelling in him just as much as the believer. But the former never calls upon God because he lacks faith that He is there, while the latter is conscious through his faith that God is with him, speaking to him, inspiring him. The classical Christian notion of *Prevenient Grace* is very important here. Prevenient grace is that grace which goes before, and acts in our lives before we believe. Since we are unaware of its existence we do not know how to cooperate with it. Many a man sweats and groans through the inspiration that comes to him by prevenience when he might greatly expand upon what is given him through recognition of its source, and, thus, cooperate with God.

Someone is always pointing out a prominent unbeliever of great attainments and a Christian of mediocre ones as an indication that Christianity is meaningless in our lives today. But no one asks what difference a lively Christian faith of the kind, for instance, Dag Hammarskjold possessed would have made in the life and accomplishments of the unbeliever, or what the life of the mediocre believer might have been without the faith.

When Moses perceived God as the basis of all existence, he made it possible for every man to know and recognize God within him. It has been more than 3,000 years since Moses lived, yet we are just beginning to grasp what God revealed to him in the burning bush: a revelation which forever changed man's relationship to his Creator. What Moses perceived was demonstrated and fulfilled in Christ, and still we are reluctant to believe it. We cannot seem to grasp that the God who set the heavens ablaze knows of and is concerned about our hangnails. Moses saw God behind everything that was, is, and is to come.

If we read the actions of Moses interpreted into our ways of thinking and acting, we see that he was anything but the weak dependent cripple that critics of religion characterize the faithful to be. When he finally acknowledged and accepted, if reluctantly, the partnership God offered him he became an amazing leader and an unbelievable source of strength for his people. Anyone who believes that surrender to God and dependence on Him makes a cripple of one has simply never gone to the mat with Him. Ask Jacob (Gen. 32:24-31).

Discussion Guide

As we read in this chapter some of the transcription of the wordless voice speaking to Moses, God tells us a great deal about himself, some of it old and some of it very new. Below is such a transcription.

> God spoke to Moses and said, 'I am the Lord. I appeared to Abraham, Isaac, and Jacob as God Almighty. But I did not let myself be known to them by my name Jehovah.
>
> Moreover, I made a covenant with them to give them Canaan, the land where they settled for a time as foreigners.
>
> And now I have heard the groaning of the Israelites, enslaved by the Egyptians, and I have called my covenant to mind.
>
> Say therefore to the Israelites, "I am the Lord. I will release you from your labours in Egypt. I will rescue you from slavery there. I will redeem you with arm outstretched and with mighty acts of judgement.
>
> I will adopt you as my people, and I will become your God. You shall know that I, the Lord, am your God, the God who releases you from your labours in Egypt.
>
> I will lead you to the land which I swore with

uplifted hand to give to Abraham, to Isaac and to Jacob, I will give it you for your possession. I am the Lord." '

(Exod. 6:2-8 NEB)

As you meditate on this passage try to see how many different things God tells us about himself. Can you see almost one for each sentence? Incidentally, the Jehovah in the text is a way of transliterating the name of God He revealed to Moses, "I AM." Try to think what kind of difference it would make in our lives if we believe the good things God tells Moses about himself and we live as if they were true. It would be some difference, wouldn't it?

4

The Bible and Its Sources

It is perplexing and sometimes discouraging to read, "Thus saith the Lord," followed by certain specific pronouncements, and then, perhaps in the very next chapter see the same introduction followed by contradictory pronouncements. There are two reasons for this. First, God speaks in the circumstances of our current human history, which make varying pronouncements necessary from time to time. Second, the Bible is a product of different writers and editors. Genesis through 2 Kings has at least four major contributors widely varying in geographic location and at least 600 years apart in time. To illustrate how this is possible, the author of Genesis 1:28, writing in the fifth century B.C. looks at the pitiful remnant returning to Jerusalem from Babylon, faced with so much work, hears God say, "Be fruitful and increase, fill the earth and subdue it" (NEB). By projection he knows this was God's command at the beginning, when humanity was just developing.

However, what does our history in the last quarter of the twentieth century find God saying to us? Is He not rather saying to us, "Watch out. Your population is exploding so rapidly that you are outstripping the capacity of the earth to feed you. The resources you need are being depleted at an alarming rate. Bring your increase into balance with the capacity of the earth to accommodate you." This chapter elaborates on these principles.

The departure of the Hebrew tribes from Egypt, their deliverance through the waters of the Red Sea and their subsequent meanderings through the desert are known, in the jargon of theologians, as the Exodus event. It is the event, more than anything else, that gave birth to the religion we know today as Judaism; indeed if there had not been an Exodus event, Israel would have remained just another nomadic tribe, unknown or forgotten. The miraculous deliverance from Egypt, the rescue from the forces of the Pharaoh, the power of God manifested when horse and chariot foundered, all helped to establish Israel as a worshiping community.

The great sensitivity to the power of God, the mind-set that produced intimate communication with Him, the worship itself sprang from faith in the omnipotence of the one God who could engineer this event. The impression of it was such that it colored the religious development in both directions from the Exodus itself, causing those who recorded and edited the history prior to that time to do so in the light of faith in one God.

These historians attributed to those living before the Exodus a faith they never actually possessed. Those living afterwards, however, were constantly reminded that the Lord God of their fathers, the God of Abraham, Isaac, and Jacob had made a covenant with them; that if they heard His words and obeyed His commandments, they would be His people and He would be their God. The oldest phrase in the Bible which comes to us in unchanged form is most probably the one below which goes back to the Exodus event itself.

> I will sing to the Lord, for he has risen up in triumph; the horse and his rider he has hurled into the sea. (Exod. 15:1 NEB)

The importance of the Exodus event is illustrated by this very simple outline frequently used to show the basic structure of the Bible.

The Prologue: Genesis 1-11

This section deals with basic origins and characteristics of all men, beginning with the creation narratives. It closely follows the account of the fall, the increasing wickedness of man, and the promise of God's deliverance of the righteous in the account of Noah and the flood. The tower of Babel showing the confusion engendered by human sin, brings this section to a close.

The Setting: Genesis 12-50

Moving from the general (all mankind) to the specific (Abraham and his descendants) this block of material shows the choosing of Israel as God's people, the growth of Abraham's descendants into the twelve tribes of Israel, their migration to Egypt and settlement there.

The Saga of Redemption: Exodus through the Revelation

Beginning with the enslavement of the children of Israel in Egypt, and describing their deliverance from it in the Exodus event, this division includes all the rest of the Bible. The redeeming power of the Exodus event is manifested over and over again in what follows in the Old Testament, while the New Testament, beginning with an account of what theologians call the Christ event, shows the power of God redeeming the New Israel, the Christian Church.

There is much to be said for this arrangement. For one thing, it has the two Testaments together, as indeed they must be.

The Old Testament without the New is an account of an unfulfilled promise, while the New Testament without the Old is a tale begun in the middle. The Bible is a unity, and therefore, no study of it that does not do justice to this reality is adequate. This unity comes from the nature of the community that created it.

Although many pens contributed to the writing and editing, these writers all had a common faith in the one God who brought about their deliverance from Egypt and who, one day, would send His Messiah, His Anointed One, to bring in the day of the Lord to man on earth. This common faith, however, is experienced by many varied human souls, living as many centuries apart, in the extremes, as we are today from the birth of Christ. The writing and editing alone span at least a thousand more. So it is obvious that many different personalities, points of view, historical backgrounds, and cultural changes are interpreting this common faith, which makes for confusing and even contradictory expressions that appear sometimes on the same page.

Nowhere is this more evident than in the section of the Bible beginning with Genesis and ending with the Second Book of Kings. In writing this book I had hoped to avoid technical critical discussions, but since the aim of this work is to interest you in an active use of the holy Scriptures, I believe it will be helpful to identify the main contributors to this section of the Old Testament, to explain how we distinguish them from each other and to discuss their differing points of view.

This brings me to some mysterious initials. J E D and P have plagued several generations of theological students. Each initial stands for an author or a group of authors or editors who made major contributions to the books mentioned. Six centuries separate the first from the last in the actual writing, and widely differing historical settings affect their points of view. One of my most vivid memories of my seminary training was the tedious task of underlining the J passages in red, those from E in blue, D in green and P in black. On occasion one might find three different contributors to a single verse.

How could these passages be separated with this kind of precision? While scholars may differ in the details, in the main they agree in their identification of these various writers. Let me explain it in this way. Suppose English were written exactly as each person pronounces it. It would be possible to distinguish easily between the writing of a native of Brooklyn and that of a native of Birmingham. Moreover, we can just as easily distinguish between the English of Chaucer and the English of Churchill. Languages in their more primitive stages tend to be spelled by the whim of the writer, rather than by any set of common rules, and while later editors tend to standardize spelling, enough identifying remarks remain to separate times and regions from each other. While these differences don't appear too obviously in King James English, the difference in the points of view does appear and makes this early part of the Old Testament sometimes quite confusing and difficult.

I have put off as long as I can the task of introducing you to the owners of these four initials. J stands for the Jahwist, because the only word he ever uses for God is Jahweh. His southern accent places him in Judah (the southern kingdom) and his archaic speech places him in the ninth century B.C. His material came from the oral traditions of the southern tribes. It must be remembered that while what we call the Holy Land is roughly the size and shape of Vermont, geographical barriers and a disinclination to travel far separated the northern and southern tribes so that their oral traditions, although of common origin, tended to differ in detail.

An example of this is the account of Hagar's experience with the Lord in the desert. Read all of Genesis 16 and then read Genesis 21:9-21. The former is from the pen of the Jahwist. It describes Hagar as a sullen and rebellious Bedouin maiden, contemptuous of Sarai, her mistress who, while pregnant, runs off into the desert and meets the angel of the Lord there by a well.

The parallel version by E is in the latter passage. In this account the child, Ishmael, has already been born and he is contemptuous of Isaac, so Hagar is driven, frightened and whimpering into the desert by Abraham at Sarah's request, and there, threatened by death from thirst, she separates herself from Ishmael and is weeping when the angel appears to her. It is only then that God opens her eyes and she sees the well. Finally, note the similarities in what might be called the punch line. In both cases Ishmael is designated by God to be the father of a great nation. Elsewhere in the Bible we realize that the Hebrews believed that Ishmael became the father of the Arab nations. The hostility today between Israel and the Arabs is of long standing as the poem by the Jahwist in Genesis 16:12 testifies.

Since I have above introduced a passage from E, I had better identify him. He is a northerner, a slightly later contemporary of J. His material comes from the verbal tradition of the northern kingdom. In his writing he uses Elohim as the name for God until the specific name, Jahweh, is revealed to Moses in the burning bush. Hence the initial E stands for the Elohist. J and E are responsible for preserving in written form the earliest verbal traditions that survive. Their work, independent of each other, is often parallel, agreeing in essence if not in detail.

It remained for D to put J and E together into a single work, together with his own material. D stands for the Deuteronomic editors and refers to the group of religious reformers who produced the book of the law found in the temple about 621 B.C. (2 Kings 22:8). This is our book of Deuteronomy (*deuteros* = second, *nomos* = law). It was quite common in the ancient world to express one's opinion on a weighty matter and then attribute the work to an ancient worthy, as these reformers, in this case, attributed their work to Moses. There was no moral problem involved here, as their conviction was then that what the book contained is indeed what Moses would have written had he been living in their time; therefore, why not make his thought known? The presumptuousness of the whole practice somehow escaped the ancients, and, as has been said, this was often done.

This group of reformers came into being just prior to the time that Judah was led off captive by the Babylonians in 599-587 B.C. It is quite possible that their efforts bolstered the badly sagging religion of the time and furnished the spiritual stamina that enabled Judah to withstand the captivity and maintain her identity during this terrible time of trial. The Deuteronomic editors not only produced the second book of the law, but also compiled and edited the material that was known as the "former prophets" (those holy men who walked through the pages of the Old Testament from Genesis through 2 Kings) using the material of J and E and other sources, some of which later became 1 and 2 Chronicles.

These editors, as far as we can tell, did not alter or delete ancient material, but simply put it together, interlining it with their own comments, which then became part of the text. As one understands those issues which concerned these reformers, an amateur can sometimes make a fairly good guess as to what is original material and what is editorial comment. While the ordinary reader will not have the discernment in this matter of the Hebrew scholar, he can develop a kind of working sense which will make these parts of the Old Testament much more intelligible to him.

If you would like to see how these editors operate, a good example is the account of Saul being made king, starting with the beginning of chapter 8 of 1 Samuel. The whole of it is written, or adapted, by D. As we read this chapter it would seem that the writer believes the desire for a king was a rejection of the kingship of the Lord. This reflects the thinking of the Deuteronomic editors who blamed all of Judah's troubles on the fact that they were ruled by kings rather than by God himself. The chapter ends with God's somewhat impatient and disapproving command for Samuel to make them a king.

Chapter 9, probably from the pen of J, shows an entirely different attitude on the part of both Samuel and the Lord. In it the Lord has clearly chosen Saul to be not only Israel's king but also the deliverer of the people. Now it is quite obvious that God, who changes not, could not have two such different opinions about the same matter. Small wonder the inexperienced reader is confused. Nevertheless, it is important to remember that both authors are steeped in the faith engendered by the Exodus event, but that the Jahwist is recounting the crowning of Saul from the tradition that was handed down from the event itself, but writing from the point in the history of Israel when most of the experience with the monarchy had been good, at a time probably very shortly after Saul, David and Solomon had reigned. He would certainly see no reason to tamper with the tradition which showed the appointment of Saul as divine origin, for the God who delivered Israel out of Egypt would certainly continue to provide for the nation through a strong king.

The Deuteronomists, however, lived at the end of a long period of very weak kings, during which the monarchy had been disastrous for Judah, and believed it completely out of character for the God who delivered Israel out of Egypt to favor providing them with a king. So D, also, speaks in terms of his theological interpretation of history, putting his thoughts in God's mouth.

But if this represents the way that God is quoted, how can we believe anyone who says "Thus saith the Lord"? The thesis of this book is that these are streaks of light, and while God may indeed speak, He is not responsible for those of us who misquote Him. Both these authors have common faith—God will save His people. And God assures both that this is true. But we are all guilty of attributing to God more than He tells us. The original concept of Saul's kingship was that it was the means by which God intended to save Israel from political weakness and confusion, which seemed to have been accomplished in J's time. The Deuteronomist's concept of the same event was that the kingship of Saul could only have been established with a concurrent disregard for the kingship of the Almighty. What God might have been saying to both is that the prosperity and well-being of a people is best assured by a ruler who leads strongly and surely, always aware of the account of his leadership he must make to the Lord.

There is one further thing worthy of note in this section. In 1 Samuel 9:12 reference is made to Samuel's offering sacrifice "in the high place" (KJV). The high places were the centers of Canaanite fertility worship and even a prophet of the standing of Samuel was involved in what was known as syncretism, the practice of incorporating, in this case, certain practices of the fertility cults into the religion of Israel. The Deuteronomic reformers abhorred this practice. In 1 Kings 14:23 they sneered at syncretism, saying "They also built them high places, and images and groves, on every high hill and under every green tree" (KJV). In other passages they refer to this practice as "whoring after other gods." Certainly, if it were not for some strong prohibition against doing so, they would have deleted this reference to high places in connection with Samuel, who was one of the ancient prophets of whom they approved. Therefore, we can be quite certain about the high degree of integrity they applied in preserving ancient material.

At last we have arrived at P. This final initial stands for the priestly editors, who, working in the fifth century B.C. and later, further edited the J E D material. Their greatest contributions were a large part of the first eleven chapters of Genesis, and almost all of the book of Leviticus. However, they can be seen elsewhere, underscoring points which further their particular interest. This group grew out of strong cultic emphases which characterized the Jews in the period of exile in Babylon. Worship served as a rallying point for these miserable, homesick Jews. Their religious fervor, which made the Jews in exile somewhat like a monastic community, drew a remnant of them ever closer together and increased the desire within them to return to Jerusalem and restore temple worship. One of the great prophets of this period was Ezekiel, whose immense power and narrow nationalism inspired the development of the priestly editors. However, this group did not actually rise up until after the return to the Holy Land, and it grew up out of the enthusiasm generated by the rebuilding of the temple under Ezra.

Their interest, in contrast to that of D, was not as much moralistic as it was cultic. They centered their concerns on matters of religious observance. An interesting example of this may be found in Genesis 1:1 through 2:3. This is the priestly account of the creation, magnificent in its scope and profound in its theological insight. Yet, notice how definitely and carefully it is said that God himself established the Sabbath by resting from His labors of creation. Long after the complex system of Sabbath observance had grown up, the priestly writers provided the authority for it by including the Sabbath of the Almighty in their account of creation.

Contrast this with the account of creation by the Jahwist, Genesis 2:4-24, excluding verses 8 through 17. Here is a much less sophisticated, much less knowledgeable account of creation, lacking the theological subtlety of the later priestly account. In J's account, Adam was made before the other animals, and then, as God made all the other animals, He brought them to Adam to be named, hoping that one among them might be suitable for a companion and helpmate. However, this desert dweller omitted from his account the creation of fish, because he was ignorant of their existence.

So here we have an example of the pattern followed by the priestly editors, namely, creating a newer version to correct and supplement the old, updating its theological content and correcting its doctrine. This was the motive for priestly editing. Another characteristic of P is the furnishing of geneological transitions from one section to another. He is the author of some of the "begats" which have effectively discouraged Bible reading for many generations. However, P intended them not only to form a useful historical framework by which the passage of time could be delineated, but also a line of inheritance by which authority, especially priestly authority, could be established.

The first eleven chapters of Genesis are heavily edited by P and, as has been suggested above, might be considered as a prologue for the whole Bible. Thereafter, with the exception of the book of Leviticus, the priestly editors are much less active, dealing only with what concerns them directly. Their hand can be seen, for example, in Genesis 17:9-14, the account of Abram's covenant with God which requires the circumcision of all males eight days after birth. Another example is to be found in Genesis 26:35 in which the priestly editor, wishing to establish a precedent forbidding marriages outside the nation, indicates the grief Isaac and Rebecca suffered when Esau, their son, takes foreign women to be his wives. In the account of the Exodus event itself, P has interjected numerous comments providing for the celebration of the Passover and the Feast of the Unleavened Bread (see Exod. 11:9-12:20). And so it goes, with the priestly editors inserting into the J E D document authority for the cultic practices they advocated.

I cannot emphasize too strongly that it was the Exodus event that created Israel as a worshiping community and held the tribes together through three centuries of guerrilla warfare during the period of Joshua and the Judges. Faith in the mighty God who could deliver them from the hand of the Egyptians inspired the establishment of Israel as a strong political unit, caused the song and saga of the community to be rewritten to reflect this faith, which is caught in the bold and vigorous prose of the Jahwist and almost a century later in the straightly moral cadences of the Elohist. The prophets called and recalled the community back to the grateful worship of Jahweh who saved them. The Deuteronomists, harking again back to the event, made Israel the people of the Torah, the Book of the Law. The priestly writers assured forever the commemoration of the event in rite and ceremony, as the Old Israel moved down through history to provide the ground for the creation of the New.

Discussion Guide

Now that you have made the acquaintance of J E D and P, I am going to quote four biblical passages in the order they appear in the Bible. See if you can identify the source.

God blessed the seventh day and made it holy, because on that day he ceased from all the work he had set himself to do.

(Gen. 2:3 NEB)

So she sat some way off, weeping bitterly. God heard the child crying, and the angel of God called from heaven to Hagar.

(Gen. 21:16-17 NEB)

All nations on earth shall pray to be blessed as your descendants are blessed, and this because you have obeyed me.

(Gen. 22:18 NEB)

Hear, O Israel, the Lord is our God, one Lord, and you must love the Lord your God with all your heart and soul and strength.

(Deut. 6:4-5 NEB)

I don't pretend that reading the previous chapter made you an instant expert, so I will comment on the answers. The first passage is from P, and the clue is that it gives authority for the observance of the Sabbath. Its concern is cultic and therefore, priestly. The second is from E as page 38 which tells you that in the E version Hagar is "frightened and whimpering." The third is J, which you could only know by realizing that this is ancient form of God's covenant with Abraham. And finally, the give-away for D is that the passage is from Deuteronomy, which is entirely by D, but also that it is highly moralistic, a kind of cornerstone of all morality.

A word should be said about the structure of the Bible as set forth in this chapter. It would be worth your time to scan quickly the prologue, the first eleven chapters of the Bible and see that they concern all mankind and deal with mankind's predicament as a result of his choosing to disobey God and learning to distinguish between good and evil. A pattern of redemption is set forth in the account of Noah and the flood, a pattern which shows God taking the initiative in saving man and His willingness to make a covenant with him. This is characteristic of God's redemptive action throughout the rest of the Bible. Then flip quickly through Genesis 12-50 and see how God sets the stage for His redemptive action, first by choosing a people to whom He will reveal His plan in a special way. We see the patriarchs responding to God's call. We also see God turn the envy of Joseph's brethren into the setting of the stage for the redemption of Israel. The end of the sin of Joseph's brothers is bondage for all Israel. Beginning with Exodus we have the unfolding of God's redeeming activity. Everything we read in this book from now on will deal with that activity. So, read on.

5

The Second Revolution of Moses

This chapter brings together two concepts which have been in the minds of men since they have been men, and somehow coexisted without being related to each other. The first of these is the experience of the holy, which seems to have been innate in man regardless of the environment from which he emerged. The other is the sense of right and wrong behavior which developed accepted customs and mores in even the most primitive societies. It is our purpose in this chapter to see how Moses, as an innovator in religion, brought these two human experiences into relationship.

This endeavor will necessarily require that we revisit the Ten Commandments and see them through twentieth-century eyes.

The singing died down from the triumphal song of Miriam celebrating the Exodus event, and the children of Israel journeyed three days into the wilderness of Shur (Exod. 15:21-24). They reached bitter waters of Marah and could not drink. And Moses spoke to the Lord and the Lord showed him how to sweeten the waters by throwing in a log from a certain tree. Whether God reminded Moses of some forgotten bit of desert lore, or whether, as Exodus 15:25

suggests, God revealed it to him at that moment is not important. What God says to him in the next verse is of utmost importance, for it is here that the second religious revolution of Moses begins.

Men, for thousands of years, long before they were able to write down their history, have been struck by feelings of awe and wonder before that which they do not understand, but that which is of immense importance to them. Whether it is majestic beauty of the mountains, the splendor of the rolling sea, the awesome power of the storm, the miracle of birth, or the sight of a dead body which causes this feeling to strike the pit of the stomach, it is what we call in our vernacular today a gut reaction. While it is akin to fear, it is not fear. Dead men are the least dangerous of men, yet the sight of a lifeless body which once talked and laughed with you produces this feeling. It seized the cave dweller in southern France and Spain and caused him to ponder the means by which some benevolent deity fed them, so they drew huge figures of the animals they ate on the walls of their caves, hoping to remain in favor with the gods of the animals and to continue to hunt them for food.

Nor was it confined to men of prehistory. The mountains, the sea, the storm, the birth of children, the death of a friend still produce these feelings in us. In our finer moments, when we take time to be sensitive to these things, we find occasions for these strange and sometimes frightening feelings greatly multiplied. They come not only as products of the wonder of God in nature but they may, also, be produced by God acting in man. During World War II, after a six-month stretch at sea in the Central Pacific, I was ashore in Honolulu carrying my Heifetz recording of Beethoven's D Major Violin Concerto under my arm, hoping to find a record player to take to sea on the next long voyage.

Finally, at the end of a long day, I found one, a poor, beat-up machine that was priced at $150.00. I put the scherzo on to try it out. I can still hear it; and as I write these words the tears that gushed out then are close to the surface now. I bought the machine.

This feeling has a name. It is called the sense of the numinous. It is this feeling that motivates us to worship. Occasionally, we may experience it in church.

There is another equally ancient sense which originally was not identified at all with religion. For convenience we will call it a sense of "oughtness" and "oughtnotness." It developed out of man's coming together in a tribal culture. Usually it existed alongside the sense of the numinous, but was not identified with it. An example of this is in the behavior of the Greek gods who were completely amoral in what they did. They contrived, they stole, they cheated, they lied, they murdered and yet they were the deities of a very highly sophisticated (we are indebted to them even for that word) people. They also gave us some of the most highly developed ethical systems men have devised. Yet their gods are without a sense of oughtness and oughtnotness.

No sooner had Moses thrown the sweetening wood into the bitter pool of Marah than he heard the wordless voice:

> He said, 'If only you will obey the Lord your God, if you will do what is right in his eyes, if you will listen to his commands and keep all his statutes, then I will never bring upon you any of the sufferings which I brought on the Egyptians; for I the Lord am your healer.'
>
> (Exod. 15:26 NEB)

and he got it all together.

And then it came to Moses, "to hearken and to do that which is right," to listen and to obey, meant (to him) that the God he recognized in the storm, the God who dwells in the volcano, the God of his father, of Abraham, Isaac, and Jacob, the God who is the author of all existence, *is a righteous God who cares how man behaves.* So first the sense of the numinous and the sense of oughtness and oughtnotness were discovered both to be attributes of God Almighty.

At this point in history the relationship between religion and morality was established. And this discovery is the basis of the title of this chapter, the second religious revolution of Moses. This relationship has been hinted at vaguely in other religions, but never before had it had the explicit expression Moses gave to it in the Ten Commandments. So much is God concerned about the behavior of men that He has created morality into His universe. When I teach the Ten Commandments to children, I liken these laws to the law of gravity which was created into the world for man to discover and hence was not the product of human legislation. This removes the commandments from our ordinary concept of immediate and specific punishments for specific infractions. In God's law the punishment as well as the law is part of the creation. For example, anyone foolish enough to violate the law of gravity is likely to break his neck in the process.

Not so obvious, perhaps, but just as devastating is the misery that results from the violation of the laws of love. Therefore it is to be hoped that as men grow in grace, they increasingly cease to think of the commandments in the category of human law, so that these precepts are obeyed because attitudes have been developed that recognize their positive contributions to life, rather than obedience through fear of punishment, with its attendant question as to whether the punishment might be an adequate price to pay for the pleasures or benefits of disobedience.

The commandments certainly merit our scrutiny of them individually. We print them below as they appear in the New English Bible.

God spoke, and these were his words: I am the Lord your God who brought you out of Egypt, out of the land of slavery. You shall have no other god to set against me.

You shall not make a carved image for yourself nor the likeness of anything in the heavens above, or on the earth below, or in the waters under the earth. You shall not bow down to them or worship them; for I, the Lord your God, am a jealous god. I punish the children for the sins of the fathers to the third and fourth generations of those who hate me. But I keep faith with thousands, with those who love me and keep my commandments.

You shall not make wrong use of the name of the Lord your God; the Lord will not leave unpunished the man who misuses his name.

Remember to keep the sabbath day holy. You have six days to labour and do all your work. But the seventh day is a sabbath of the Lord your God; that day you shall not do any work, you, your son or your daughter, your slave or your slave-girl, your cattle or the alien within your gates; for in six days the Lord made heaven and earth, the sea, and all that is in them, and on the seventh day he rested. Therefore the Lord blessed the sabbath day and declared it holy.

Honour your father and your mother, that you may live long in the land which the Lord your God is giving you.

You shall not commit murder.

You shall not commit adultery.

You shall not steal.

You shall not give false evidence against your neighbour.

You shall not covet your neighbour's house; you shall not covet your neighbour's wife, his slave, his slave-girl, his ox, his ass, or anything that belongs to him. (Exod. 20:1-17 NEB)

If we insist on holding to our rewards-punishment mentality, as we all do to an extent, the first commandment quite adequately illustrated the principle of the built-in punishments.

"You shall have no other God to set against me." If there is only one God and if He alone is almighty, all-knowing and all-loving, then by making a god of an entity who does not possess these attributes, we would be worshiping a being who lacks the power, knowledge and love by which to fulfill our needs. To worship such a deity condemns one to a frustration and futility which is punishment enough.

If this is so, how much greater punishment results from the worship of the works of our hands: a golden calf, a bottle of booze, or a dollar bill. From the point of view of a Christian, to worship such is unrealistic. From the point of view of the desert dwelling Israelite, the matter is more personal. He attributes the disaster which comes to the jealousy of God. But we can see that the transgressor is not punished by an angry God but he is broken on the reality of the law, just as surely as the suicide who jumps from a tall building is broken on the law of gravity.

The third commandment was the one I had the greatest difficulty fitting into this pattern, which is most familiarly expressed, "Thou shalt not take the name of the Lord thy God in vain." At first it seemed rather petty to me for the Almighty to take such a dim view of swearing, particularly when there were such grave provocations like hitting your thumb with a hammer. But then I gradually realized that the problem wasn't God's—it was mine. If I really didn't want Him to damn the hammer into hell for all eternity, I'd best not ask Him to do so, lest I be in the position of the boy calling "Wolf!" Taking the Lord's name in vain messes up your prayers, which means it chops off communication between you and the Lord. *That* is penalty enough.

Most clergymen think the fourth commandment doesn't apply to them. Somehow or another, we reason, if we are not actually God's partners in creation, we are, at the very least, His partners in salvation: the world isn't going to be saved unless we uphold our end. One of the devil's surest means of destroying a man of the cloth is to convince him that he is exempt from one of the commandments so that he needn't practice what he preaches. This reasoning doesn't fool the most obtuse layman in a congregation, but it is sure-fire in fooling the preacher. "Six days shalt thou labor, . . ." What a piece of wisdom! Many young ministers come to me soured on their work, discontented with their people, hating the ministry. My consultation with them runs something like this:

"What day do you take off during the week?"

"Oh, I'm much too busy to take a day off. There are too many demands."

"Don't you know you can do more work in six days than in seven?"

"But there is just too much."

"Who exempted you from the fourth commandment?"

"Oh—"

I know. I was just an eyelash from the loony bin before I discovered that God's laws apply to clergymen and professional religious as much as to anyone else.

"Honor thy father and thy mother." With the beating that poor old mom and dad have been taking lately, it would seem that the mental health people and the social scientists have repealed this one. But I think this fable I manufactured about Joe Glotz might be revealing.

Joe Glotz was married at seventeen and in the two years since, Joe had produced two children and had worked at seven different jobs with periods of unemployment between each. However, "Now," says Joe, "my troubles are over. This is the best job I ever had. For the first time I have a boss who really understands me. I'm looking forward to starting to work tomorrow."

Two weeks pass and poor Joe has changed his tune. "How's the new boss, Joe?"

"That bum—"

In less than a hundred words about him those of us who deal with such people can diagnose Joe's trouble. Joe has an authority problem which probably dates from his inability to honor his father and mother. He has not learned to honor and respect the authority put over him for its own sake, without regard for the kind of authority it is. Respect for lawfully constituted authority in no way abridges one's right to protest or dissent when such is required. But the inability to accept any authority is an almost insuperable burden, a terrible price to pay for not honoring one's father and one's mother, thereby failing to learn to accept authority however little those in authority may deserve the honor. If nothing else, it was through them God gave you life. If living means anything to you, you can honor your parents for that.

Some of the commandments resemble icebergs, with only an eighth showing above the surface and the other seven-eighths of each being discovered only as disaster reveals them. So it is with "Thou shalt not kill." Generations of English speaking peoples, especially those who have felt the influence of the Book of Common Prayer, have taken solace in the earlier translation, "Thou shalt do no murder" (also the way the New English Bible has it) which seems to exempt capital punishment, war, justified homicide, and other costly violations from judgment.

Certainly the children of Israel saw it this way: the "life for life" principle is enunciated in the very next chapter of Exodus. Moreover, the enemies of Israel were looked upon as the enemies of Jahweh and killing was too good for them. Remember how the prophet Samuel ". . . hewed Agag in pieces before the Lord in Gilgal" (1 Sam. 15:33)? But the truth is that God often spoke to men in Scripture more clearly than they were able to hear, and it has remained for future generations to understand what had been said to previous ones.

An example of this truth is the first-century attitude toward the institution of human slavery. Saint Paul obviously accepted it as did his whole social environment, and even though he had many edifying things to say about how slave and master need to treat each other as Christians, I find no condemnation by him of the institution of slavery. That condemnation was 1800 years in coming into the Christian point of view.

So it is with the sixth commandment. Increasingly insistent voices are being raised against both capital punishment and wars as violations, extremely costly ones, of the commandment. I went with some conviction, and certainly without any qualms of conscience, as a volunteer in the Navy during World

War II. The events and brushfire wars of subsequent years are changing my mind concerning the value of war. My son has already made up his. Below is an excerpt of a statement he sent to what I predicted was a somewhat bemused draft board.

A basic premise of Christianity is that Christians are to pattern their own lives after that of Christ, that, in any given situation, they are to behave as Christ would in the same situation. How so many Christians delude themselves into imagining Christ trooping off to battle, gun in hand, prepared to take the life of his own creation is beyond my feeble mind, but, somehow, I cannot rationalize myself into picturing Him doing so. What would nationalism and patriotism mean to Christ as compared to a single human life? Consider Christ, head shaved, helmeted and camouflaged, with ammo-belts and hand grenades hanging on his body, gun poised and finger fidgeting on the trigger as he levels the cross in the sights between the almond eyes of some unwary oriental but, nevertheless, human face. There is an explosion, a bullet is discharged, and almost immediately it hideously disfigures the head and mind of an imperfect image of God himself. Would He blow off the muzzle and laud the attributes of apple pie, and while calming himself with thoughts of the Statue of Liberty, sigh and say, "My country, right or wrong," or would he commit suicide, or would he be in that situation in the first place? He wouldn't and I won't either.

While all the sentiments therein are not necessarily the opinions of the paternal management, I find myself hard put for an answer to the question he raises. Moreover, there is no more vivid example of the wrath of God vented in punishment for human sin than in the devastation, tragedy, and idiotic waste of war. Worse, however, is the transfiguration of those who worship at the altar of Mars. Certainly the bestiality resulting from this idolatry is visited on the children unto the third and fourth generation.

"Thou shalt not commit adultery." Here is another commandment which is taking a real beating in an age of great permissiveness, encouragement coming from the Playboy attitudes toward sex and the swingers all around us. It is an age of great frankness and openness about sex and this is a good thing. I will be candid. Adultery to me means dilution. When you adulterate milk or alcohol you add water to it. This is the problem about adultery. It dilutes things that ought to be full strength. After a particularly sensitive and beautiful episode of lovemaking with my wife which was filled with communication of a marvelous and unbelievable sort, I mused to myself, "How would you ever learn to do that without twenty-eight years of practice!" I believe God wants the best for us. So you may dilute your sex if you like. I'll take mine straight.

I suppose nothing got a cave man into trouble faster than to steal the favorite spear of his neighbor. So it has been ever since. God does not need circumstances to be the rod of His anger, as is the case in idolatry—human indignation does quite well as an avenger. However, we do need to ponder the enormous variety of things which can be stolen. The real argument against human slavery is that it robs a man both of his freedom and the fruits of his labor. What a long time it took us to see it! There is also the over-protective parent who robs his child of his confidence. What a terrible theft, and yet how common! I suppose none of us could survive a session of rigorous self-examination without awareness that we have taken something that does not belong to us. "Thou shalt not steal." How far removed it sounds, pointing the accusing finger at felons who are in prisons and perhaps at politicians who ought to be. We never seem to notice that finger pointed at ourselves, yet how near guilt is.

Still, the commandment most often broken by the respectable, middle-class (often self-righteous) churchgoer is the ninth: "Thou shalt not bear false witness against thy neighbor." This shoots the arrow right into the heart of that favorite indoor sport—gossip. The contention, if it has not come through clearly, of this whole section on the commandments, is that the punishment is built into the transgression and is an inevitable consequence of it. In the case of false witness in a court which condemned an innocent person, there surely must be a constant imprint of that innocent's suffering on the mind of the witness, as close and constant as breathing. With the gossip, however, there comes a coarsening of viewpoint, an inability to see the good because of preoccupation with the search for the evil, a distortion which corrupts all it sees. In the process of storytelling, the gossiper not only loses credibility, but no one will want to expose himself to the predatory glance of the slanderer. I suppose gossips develop enough paranoia to compensate for the loneliness they unconsciously (or consciously) feel.

It took me the longest time to see why one should not covet. "What *is* the matter," I reasoned, " with wanting something that someone else has. Perhaps this desire a person has will produce the ambition in him to work hard to obtain the object for himself." Then I coveted that which was obtainable only through destruction and I knew. To covet is to poison the mind as to the value of what you already have, to torment yourself by thinking of what you cannot have, or perhaps to tempt you to break some of the other commandments to get what you want. It produces a misery that makes contentment impossible, and places happiness well beyond reach, and puts joy out of the question. Covetousness is a cheerless proposition and I can't for the life of me see how it has such widespread support.

In considering these commandments which God led Moses to discover and bring to Israel from the mount, it is clear that God reveals to us, as He did to Moses, that He is a God who cares how men behave, a God who built these concepts into His creation so that to live contrary to them is not to experience the joy He intended but to experience the pain He did not intend. The God of the storm, who lives in the volcano, the God of Abraham, Isaac, and Jacob is indeed a God of righteousness.

Discussion Guide

We have seen that our God is a God of righteousness, that He wills that our behavior be in accordance with His nature. But we are free to obey or disobey, to do His will or disregard it. How is His will brought to bear on us? Is it in the mode of the drill sergeant who rules the recruits by the book and they do his will or else? Or is His attitude one of loving and gentle persuasion? Does He single us out personally when His displeasure is incurred? Perhaps the Psalm below offers a clue.

Psalm 100

1. Be joyful in the Lord, all you lands;
   serve the Lord with gladness
   and come before his presence with a song.
2. Know this: The Lord himself is God;
   he himself has made us, and we are his;
   we are his people and the sheep of his pasture.
3. Enter his gates with thanksgiving;

go into his courts with praise;
give thanks to him and call upon his Name.
4. For the Lord is good;
his mercy is everlasting;
and his faithfulness endures from age to age.
                    Proposed Book of Common Prayer

What can we infer from this Psalm about the way God brings His will to bear upon us? What attitudes on our part does He require? What picture of Him do we receive? How does God's attitude toward us help to shape our attitude toward Him? Perhaps you know other parts of the Old Testament that strengthen or reinforce this picture.

6

The Lion Has Roared

The people Israel saw in their national history five major ways in which God intervened and favored them above all peoples: in the calling of the patriarchs, Abraham, Isaac, and Jacob; in the deliverance from bondage in Egypt through the Red Sea; in their preservation during the forty years of wandering in the desert; in their conquest of the Promised Land; and in the golden age under David. But as they adopted more and more of the ways of the Canaanites and their worship, and their culture changed, things began to grow sour and they asked, "Why has the Lord deserted us?" The prophets were there to answer, "What can you expect? It is you who have deserted the Lord and His commandments."

The purpose of this chapter is to look at the prophetic office in terms of the tension between the power of the demand in God's call and the sense of inadequacy and unworthiness it engenders in the prophet, making him reluctant to accept it. I also wish to show that once the call to prophecy is accepted, there is a tremendous awareness of the need for absolute integrity in carrying it out.

The prophet Amos has said it for all the prophets of the Old Testament and all who have come later, follow-

ing in the biblical tradition.
> For the Lord God does nothing without giving to his servants the prophets knowledge of his plans.
>
> The lion has roared; who is not terrified? The Lord God has spoken; who will not prophesy?
>
> (Amos 3:7-8 NEB)

The injunction "to hearken and to obey" which became the basis of Moses' second revolution is intensified in the life of the prophet. The corollary of this injunction is that if the prophet disobeys, he becomes unable to hearken. It does not mean that the voice stops, but that the prophet has lost his sensitivity to it. So it happened to Gideon when he disobeyed the Lord, collected the golden jewelry of the people, and made it into a symbol of his own authority which he set up in his city. The Deuteronomist judges the act harshly with these words: "And all Israel went thither a whoring after it: which thing became a snare unto Gideon, and to his house" (Judg. 8:27 KJV).

I indicated in chapter three that I did not want to discuss Moses' reluctance to accept God's call in that chapter because I intended discussing the call of various prophets in a later chapter. The time has arrived. In the third and fourth chapters of Exodus, Moses expresses his reluctance to accept the leadership God is putting upon him by compiling quite a list of lame excuses.

> But who am I . . . that I should go to Pharaoh, and that I should bring the Israelites out of Egypt?
>
> (Exod. 3:11 NEB)

> If I go to the Israelites and tell them that the God of their forefathers has sent me to them, and they ask me his name, what shall I say?
>
> (Exod. 3:13 NEB)

> But they will never believe me or listen to me;

they will say, 'The Lord did not appear to you.'
(Exod. 4:1 NEB)

O Lord, I have never been a man of ready speech, never in my life, not even now that thou hast spoken to me; I am slow and hesitant of speech.
(Exod. 4:10 NEB)

Saint Thomas Aquinas tells us that God is devoid of passions in the human sense, but the desert Hebrew would never buy that. As Moses continued inventing excuse after excuse the celestial patience begins to wear thin.

Who is it that gives a man speech? Who makes him dumb or deaf? Who makes him clear sighted or blind? Is it not I, the Lord? Go now; I will help your speech and tell you what to say.
(Exod. 4:11-13 NEB)

But even with this unanswerable logic, Moses is still unconvinced, and he mutters something that can be paraphrased, "Send someone else who can do it better." As punishment for his reluctance, Aaron, Moses' brother, is assigned to be his mouthpiece as well.

The kind of reluctance Moses manifested before God's call is a pattern of behavior shown over and over again among the various prophets who hear it. We can also see some of the terror that is frequently part of it as exemplified by Isaiah's response.

Woe is me! I am lost, for I am a man of unclean lips and I dwell among a people of unclean lips; yet with these eyes I have seen the King, the Lord of Hosts.
(Isa. 6:5 NEB)

Jeremiah's call adds still another dimension to the burden of the prophet, that of the awesome authority of his utterance.

> The word of the Lord came to me: 'Before I formed you in the womb I knew you for my own; before you were born I consecrated you, I appointed you a prophet to the nations.' 'Ah! Lord God,' I answered, 'I do not know how to speak; I am only a child.' But the Lord said, 'Do not call yourself a child; for you shall go to whatever people I send you and say whatever I tell you to say. Fear none of them, for I am with you and will keep you safe.' This was the very word of the Lord. Then the Lord stretched out his hand and touched my mouth. . . . This day I give you authority over nations and over kingdoms, to pull down and to uproot, to destroy and to demolish, to build and to plant.'
>
> (Jer. 1:4-10 NEB)

The reaction of the prophets to the call of the Lord is typical of that of every man or woman. In my own case I remember so vividly my own reluctance, my deep sense of unworthiness, and the strong conviction that came over me that all these misgivings were irrelevant. God would supply what I lacked, and if I didn't allow Him to, if I continued to insist on my own conditions, it was so much the worse for me. I had but to listen and obey. And what has been my own experience has also been that of the young men who have come to me to discuss their own call with me. That the basis of the call has been laid long before we have any knowledge of it or part in it is certainly quite evident in the call of Jeremiah above.

The above would make it seem that only the call to the prophetic and the clerical come from God and that the ordinary layman, the person in the pew, must fend for himself. Nothing could be less true. God calls every man; the injunction to listen and to obey is universal.

There is a priesthood of all believers and each human soul is nominated and called to have his part in it. These Old Testament prophets speak to us because they describe the pattern we see confirmed by our own reluctance, our own sense of inadequacy, and yet they give us hope that if we listen hard enough and long enough to them, they strengthen our knowledge that God supplies what we lack.

As the prophet continues to listen, he forms an increasing sense of the integrity with which he must transmit the work of God as it comes to him.

Many look upon the prophets as seers or fortune tellers who do a kind of crystal ball gazing in which they accurately predict the future. This is to misunderstand their role. In a sense, the best modern equivalent to the prophet of Israel is the newspaper editor of today, who attempts to discern the course of history and point out to his reader the course events may take. However, there is one significant difference. The prophet prefaces his remarks with the authoritative phrase: "Thus saith the Lord." He is conscious of the voice of God supplying the matter of his prophecy. True to the premise of this book, this recognition of some divine authorship is a difference in consciousness of the source of the insights, rather than in the source itself. This claim, "Thus saith the Lord," is unique in the Old Testament as it applies to the matter itself, and the only parallels in the use of the claim would seem to come from some Hebrew forebears from the upper Euphrates valley (circa 1700 B.C.).*

It is quite a thing, really, for a man to come before a king or a people and, under the preface of "Thus saith the Lord," tell what none of them wants to hear. The matter of integrity comes into the picture here: the

---

*Wright and Filson, *Biblical Archeology* (Philadelphia, 1945). pp. 62-63.

discernment between the false or lying prophet and the one who speaks the word of the Lord. The standards by which this evaluation can be made are set forth early in the Old Testament, and if we find some of them in Bible passages not so well known to us, they were, nevertheless, well established in the minds of Israel.

The first instance of this devotion of the prophet to the strict pronouncement of the word of Yahweh is found, oddly enough, hidden away in the report of the census of Israel in the twenty-second through twenty-fourth chapters of the book of Numbers. As the Israelites make their way toward the Promised Land, the domains which lie across their path are threatened by this immense horde of people living off the land as they travel. Blood may in some cases be thicker than water, but in no case does one king, Balak, King of Moab, want even his distant relatives, the Israelites, licking up all that is round about him "as the ox licketh up the grass of the field." So Balak imports a prophet named Balaam to curse Israel.

Balaam is at first very reluctant to come because the commission presupposes the content of the prophecy, and he complains, "If Balak would give me his house full of silver and gold, I cannot go beyond the word of the Lord my God, to do less or more." However, the promised pay is good and perhaps the Lord will allow Balaam to prophesy in a manner satisfactory to Balak, so Balaam goes. After fulfilling all the ritual requirements, three times Balaam calls upon the Lord and three times God directs him to bless rather than to curse the Israelites.

> At that Balak was very angry with Balaam, beat his hands together and said, 'I summoned you to denounce my enemies, and three times you have persisted in blessing them.

Off with you to your own place! I promised to confer great honour upon you, but now the Lord has kept this honour from you.'

Balaam answered, 'But I told your own messengers whom you sent:

"If Balak gives me all the silver and gold in his house, I cannot disobey the command of the Lord by doing anything of my own will, good or bad. What the Lord speaks to me, that is what I will say."'

(Num. 24:10-13 NEB)

While the Bible is by no means considered a comical book, it does have its humorous passages and this whole three-chapter section is very well done. I commend it to you, not only for its clear delineation of the prophet's requirement to be true to what the Lord tells him, but also for the subtle way in which the account is given.

An even greater example of the integrity comes during the reign of David. There is probably no greater power on earth than an Oriental potentate, and David was well on his way to becoming that in the latter years of his reign. The incident with Bathsheba comes after David has reached middle age and no longer goes to the battle lines but directs the campaigns from the safety and comfort of the palace. The whole account (2 Sam. 11:1-12:23) is worthy of your time, for there is humor here mixed with irony and tragedy.

David brings the wife of Uriah the Hittite to him and she conceives by him. In order to get himself out of this predicament, David sends for Uriah, hoping to get him to sleep with his wife so that the child of David she has conceived will appear to be Uriah's. Uriah, however, gung-ho soldier that he is, refuses to do so while his companions in arms are confined to the battle zone. David, in his desperation, assigns Uriah to the forefront of the fighting so that he is killed; then he takes Bathsheba as his own wife, certain that he has gotten by with the whole business. But he has not reckoned on the prophet Nathan.

Now here is David, sole ruler of a rising force in the Middle East, with power of life or death over his subjects, and here is Nathan, knowing that, regardless of the consequences, he must accuse David of a crime against the Lord. Nathan must have pondered and prayed long before he discovered (or the Lord put into his mind) a device which would bring shame rather than anger to David's heart. The result is worthy of reproduction here.

The Lord sent Nathan the prophet to David, and when he entered his presence, he said to him, 'There were once two men in the same city, one rich and the other poor.

The rich man had large flocks and herds, but the poor man had nothing of his own except one little ewe lamb. He reared it himself, and it grew up in his home with his own sons. It ate from his dish, drank from his cup and nestled in his arm; it was like a daughter to him.

One day a traveller came to the rich man's house, and he, too mean to take something from his own flocks and herds to serve to his guest, took the poor man's lamb and served up that.'

David was very angry, and burst out, 'As the Lord lives, the man who did this deserves to die!

He shall pay for the lamb four times over, because he has done this and shown no pity.'

Then Nathan said to David, 'You are the man. This is the word of the Lord the God of Israel to you: "I anointed you king over Israel, I rescued you from the power of Saul,

I gave you your master's daughter and his wives to be your own, I gave you the daughters of Israel and Judah; and, had this not been enough, I would have added other favours as great.

Why then have you flouted the word of the Lord by doing what is wrong in my eyes? You have struck down Uriah the Hittite with the sword; the man himself you murdered by the sword of the Ammonites, and you have stolen his wife.

Now, therefore, since you have despised me and taken the wife of Uriah the Hittite to be your own wife, your family shall never again have rest from the sword."

This is the word of the Lord: "I will bring trouble upon you from within your own family; I will take your wives and give them to another man before your eyes, and he will lie with them in broad daylight.

What you did was done in secret; but I will do this in the light of day for all Israel to see."'

David said to Nathan, 'I have sinned against the Lord.' Nathan answered him, 'The Lord has laid on another the consequences of your sin: you shall not die,

But, because in this you have shown your contempt for the Lord, the boy that will be born to you shall die.'

(2 Sam. 12:1-14 NEB)

The obligation of the prophet is not only to be true to what the Lord has told him, but it is also to make every effort to be effective in calling the sinner to repentance. We certainly see, from the passage above, how effective Nathan was with David.

In passing, David's attitude over the death of his child (2 Sam. 12:15-31), while it has nothing to say about the integrity of the prophet, does say a great deal about proper penitence and acceptance of things as they are. I am afraid many of us would be mystified by the abrupt change in David's behavior after the child died. While the child was still alive he fasted and prayed that he be spared. When the child died he went about his business as usual. Yet he is quite correct. While there is hope that prayer can alter things, this is the time for praying. When that hope is past and the worst has come, that is the time for acceptance, the time to return to living life as it is now. Oceans of tears have been shed when this lesson was not learned.

The integrity of the prophet was a quality that increased in its sensitivity as time went on and the insights of the prophets increased. However, there arose a group of false prophets who attached themselves to the courts of the king, or curried favor with the people by telling them what they wanted to hear. Yet there was always that lonely figure who came before the king and spoke as the Lord had spoken to him, although he usually suffered as a result.

Such a one is Micaiah, identified only as the son of Imlah. Time after time, I have assigned the first thirty-eight verses of the twenty-second chapter of the first book of the Kings for people to read, hoping they would feel the impact of the passage and see its humor, but have usually been disappointed. So bear with me if I seem to belabor the obvious in the treatment of this section. Experience has taught me that I must.

I like to imagine the scene as this chapter opens. Here are the two kings, Ahab and Jehoshaphat, conferring together with all the pomp that must have surrounded the courts of small nations. At one moment Jehoshaphat is putting all that he has at the disposal of Ahab without reservation, and the next he has gotten cold feet and wants to hear the word of the Lord from the prophets. Ahab is well prepared and produced four hundred* to testify favorably concerning the proposed military conquest. We can imagine the place overflowing with prophets (all "yes" men), bowing and scraping and mouthing almost identical phrases: "Go up to Ramoth-gilead and conquer. The Lord shall deliver it into the king's hand." But Jehoshaphat's ambivalence continues to plague Ahab in spite of the drama and the ingenuity of the attempt of Kenaanah, one of the false prophets, to convince him by roaring about with his horns of iron, demonstrating how these will push the enemy off the mountain they have occupied.

"Is there not here a prophet of the Lord besides, that we might enquire of him?" We can sense Ahab's patience wearing thin. "There is yet one man, by whom we may enquire of the Lord; but I hate him; for he doth not prophesy good concerning me but evil." So we can presume that Ahab recognizes integrity when he hears it, even though he avoids hearing it as long as he can. The messenger is dispatched to bring this fearless prophet, Micaiah, and in order that things go right when Micaiah arrives, the messenger has a few instruc-

---

*A word needs to be said about the use of numbers in the Bible. Notice they are always nice and round and fall into certain patterns—three, seven, twelve, forty, four hundred and one hundred and forty-four thousand, etc. They are not meant to be exact, but are meant to be understood in much the way we use adjectives to describe quantity. Four hundred here means an enormous number.

tions for the prophet: "Behold now, the words of the prophets declare good unto the king with one mouth; let thy word, I pray thee, be like the word of one of them, and speak that which is good."

Micaiah replied none too reasurringly: "As the Lord liveth, what the Lord saith unto me, that will I speak."

Micaiah arrives at court and finds Ahab hostile and Jehoshaphat apprehensive. Ahab's voice has an edge as he asks the familiar question: "Shall we go up to battle or shall we forbear?"

"Go and prosper: for the Lord shall deliver it into the hand of the king."

(I love to read this passage aloud and read the response of Micaiah in a kind of mocking falsetto with which I am sure it was delivered.)

"How many times shall I adjure thee that thou tell me nothing but that which is true in the name of the Lord!" thundered Ahab. He may not have wanted the truth very badly, but he is not willing to accept a lie, even in jest, from the mouth of an honest prophet. And then the truth came.

"I saw all Israel scattered upon the hills, as sheep that have no shepherd: and the Lord said, These have no master: let them return every man to his house in peace," intoned the prophet.

"Did I not tell thee that he would prophesy no good concerning me, but evil?" Ahab muttered.

Then Micaiah tells his story:

'Listen now to the word of the Lord. I saw the Lord seated on his throne, with all the host of heaven in attendance on his right and on his left.

The Lord said, "Who will entice Ahab to attack and fall on Ramoth-gilead?" One said one thing and one said another;

Then a spirit came forward and stood before the

Lord and said, "I will entice him."

"How?" said the Lord. "I will go out," he said, "and be a lying spirit in the mouth of all his prophets." "You shall entice him," said the Lord, "and you shall succeed; go and do it."

You see, then, how the Lord has put a lying spirit in the mouth of all these prophets of yours, because he has decreed disaster for you.'

Then Zedekiah son of Kenaanah came up to Micaiah and struck him in the face: 'And how did the spirit of the Lord pass from me to speak to you?' he said.

Micaiah answered, 'That you will find out on the day when you run into an inner room to hide yourself.'

Then the king of Israel ordered Micaiah to be arrested and committed to the custody of Amon the governor of the city and Joash the king's son.

'Lock this fellow up,' he said, 'and give him prison diet of bread and water until I come home in safety.'

Micaiah retorted, 'If you do return in safety, the Lord has not spoken by me.'

(1 Kings 22:19-28 NEB)

Micaiah told the truth and was persecuted for it. Ahab was killed by the merest chance by an arrow shot at random into the Israelite forces. And prophets went on telling the truth in an illustrious succession of generations, to a variety of audiences, under many different circumstances, with all kinds of consequences. Times change and the style of prophetic utterance changes with it, from the directness of Amos to the more fanciful expression of Ezekiel to the outright fantasy of Daniel. But the integrity stayed, no matter how it was expressed. I love to read the third chapter of Daniel aloud. It is a magnificent passage of English prose, with its rolling cadences and measured phrasing. But it is easy to be seduced by the beauty of language and to neglect the content, for here again, in a different form, is expression of the integrity demanded by the most high God. The message that God will provide for those who are loyal to Him cannot be mistaken.

Hopefully, some of this prophetic office rubs off on all who are called to the ministry, clerical or lay, and at least the choices are made clear, and the call to speak as the Lord has spoken to you is there to obey or to ignore. There are many times when all of us betray our Lord through timidity or cowardice, but there are times when we do speak out. There is sometimes an overwhelming compulsion to do so, and in a sense, the issue is taken out of our hands. The prophet Amos described a real feeling when he declared:

> The lion has roared, who is not terrified? The Lord God has spoken, who will not prophesy?
>
> (Amos 3:8 NEB)

Discussion Guide

The prophets obtained from the Lord the courage to stand up and be counted. They were certainly not applauded for it. They suffered everything from extreme physical abuse to martyrdom. Amos was insulted in the middle of his oracle by Amaziah, a priest of Bethel, but it did not stop him. Consider what he has to say.

> The time is coming, says the Lord God, when I will send famine on the land, not hunger for bread or thirst for water, but for hearing the word of the Lord.

Men shall stagger from north to south, they shall range from east to west, seeking the word of the Lord, but they shall not find it.

On that day fair maidens and young men shall faint from thirst. . . .
(Amos 8:11-13 NEB)

What is God telling us through the words of Amos today? How does it relate to the principle "Listen and obey"? How would you characterize our people in terms of this oracle of Amos? How do you characterize yourself?

7

The Impertinence of Job

As God revealed himself to men, they saw Him as their vision was colored by their environment, experience, conditioning, culture, not to mention their own personal viewpoints and idiosyncrasies. So the picture we have of God in the Bible is by no means uniform, nor did the theology of the writers agree any more than the many sects of Christendom today agree in matters of theology. Certainly a minority report is found in the book of Job. The party line of Judaism, as set forth most firmly by the Deuteronomic editors, (remember D?) was that whenever you sinned, God zapped you for it quickly and completely. Therefore the greater your misfortunes the greater your sin must have been.

The writer of the book of Job denies this and the drama he produces is a refutation of the concept. It is a great credit to those who finally put together the Old Testament in its final form that dissenting views were given a hearing. There are many points of view that are not in the main stream of popular and accepted theological opinion. Isaiah 53 is one of the most important of these.

Job does something else that most men would like to do at some point in their relationship with God. He shakes his fist at Him. He gets very angry at Him, and brazenly utters impertinent things. Yet he can't escape from God. Some of the greatest poetry ever written is found in this book. I hope what this chapter has to say about it will encourage you to wade through the book. Wade is the word.

One of my students in preaching entered into a lengthy discourse on the patience of Job, which gave me an opportunity to teach a valuable lesson; namely, never preach on a book of the Bible you haven't read. Those who insist on the patience of Job have read through the prologue, which is quite clear and straightforward prose, only to flounder on the succeeding sections which are beautiful but complex and difficult poetry. While it is true that Job's utterances in the prologue do show great patience in the face of bereavement and catastrophe, this patience is soon drowned in a sea of self-pity. For example, contrast the two verses from the prologue:

The Lord gives and the Lord takes away; blessed be the name of the Lord. (Job 1:21 NEB)

'You talk as any wicked fool of a woman might talk. If we accept good from God, shall we not accept evil?' (Job 2:10 NEB)

with these taken from the beginning of the poetic section in chapter three.

Perish the day when I was born
   and the night which said, 'A man is
conceived'!

May that day turn to darkness; may
   God above not look for it,
nor light of dawn shine on it.
                    (Job 3:3-4 NEB)

It is my hope that those who read this book will do so with the Bible in hand. It will certainly make what I have written much more interesting and meaningful. However, I don't know whether I can trust you, dear reader, to do so. Therefore in order to make what follows intelligible, I include the following brief summary of the main argument of the book of Job.

Job was apparently a well-known heroic figure to the ancient world and the bare bones of this oft-told tale is in the prologue. Job was a wealthy and benevolent man, blessed with a large family and living in great prosperity and exceptional piety.

One day in heaven God and His angels were having some manner of conference which was also attended by Satan. God asked Satan whether he had observed the virtue of God's servant, Job, to which Satan contemptuously replied that Job doesn't serve God for nothing, and if God let him apply his deviltry to his possessions and family he would curse God to His face.

God gave Satan the green light, restricting him only from harming Job's person, and immediately Job lost everything. Through this, Job maintained his faithful relationship to God. Another conference was held with the same general conversation between God and Satan, and in this case God permitted Satan to bring physical suffering to Job with the sole restriction that he spare his life. Through this trial Job maintained his integrity in his relationship toward God. (I hope this summary has been sufficiently dull that you will immediately read the first two chapters of Job to see how vividly it is told in the Bible.)

At this point the author of the book leaves the old tale and begins his poetic interpretation of Job's attitude toward his misfortune, and in order to display it, uses the device of having three of Job's friends come to comfort him. Actually, the three friends represent, in various ways, the traditional theology of Judaism in connection with evil; namely, that each evil suffered in the life of a man is a direct consequence of his sin. Job denies that he has sinned, and demands justice of God. So the ministrations of the friends are scarcely comforting and largely take the position that Job's sin must be great indeed to have brought upon him such massive retribution from God.

A fourth person, Elihu, enters the scene and rebukes Job with a long-winded peroration of somewhat lesser quality than that which makes up what precedes it. Many scholars believe that this was added by a later scribe who felt that Job was not sufficiently chastened by the discourses of the three friends. Then, finally, God speaks in a whirlwind to Job, and, finally, Job sees the reality of God and himself and repents. In the end his losses are restored many fold and he lives a long, healthy, happy life.

Those are the bare bones of the account. But the beauty and power of the book are not in the story itself but rather in the skill and subtlety of the author in making his theological points. It has been hinted above that the purpose of this unknown poet in writing this work was to refute the then current, strongly entrenched notion that what an evil man suffers on earth is an immediate consequence of his sin. If this is his purpose at all, it is secondary and subordinate to other concerns.

Basically one of his concerns is to demonstrate man's sense of indignation and helplessness in his relationship with God, certainly in connection with those evils that befall him. I have called this chapter "The Impertinence of Job," and it is in his reaction to what has happened to him that the impertinence lies. He feels that God is hounding him, in spite of his efforts to please Him, and he demands justice of God and recognition of his merits, but is unwilling to concede, as St. Paul does, that "all have sinned and come short of the glory of God" (Rom. 3:23 KJV). But this impertinence of Job is the impertinence of every man. Job, tired to death of it all, at one point expresses it this way:

> Therefore I will not refrain my mouth: I will speak in the anguish of my spirit; I will complain in the bitterness of my soul.
>
> Am I a sea, or a whale, that thou settest a watch over me?
>
> When I say, My bed shall comfort me, my couch shall ease my complaint;
>
> Then thou scarest me with dreams, and terrifiest me through visions:
>
> So that my soul chooseth strangling and death rather than my life.
>
> I loathe it; I would not live alway: let me alone; for my days are vanity.
>
> What is man, that thou shouldest magnify him? and that thou shouldest set thine heart upon him?
>
> And that thou shouldest visit him every morning, and try him every moment?
>
> How long will thou not depart from me, nor let me alone till I swallow down my spittle?
> (Job 7:11-19 KJV)

> If I have sinned, how do I injure thee, thou watcher of the hearts of men? Why has thou made me thy butt, and why have I become thy target?
>
> Why dost thou not pardon my offence and take away my guilt? But now I shall lie down in the grave; seek me, and I shall not be.
> (Job 7:20-21 NEB)

I believe that any of us who have experienced a close relationship with God have said, with Job, "Let me alone!" This wish that God would get off our backs is often acute when He places some burden upon us that we feel unequal to bearing, either in terms of endurance or responsibility. The reluctance of the prophet to accept his call from God discussed in the previous chapter is expression of this wish.

Even as gentle a saint as St. Teresa of Avila has her moments of impertinence. I remember reading somewhere of a conversation she had with the Lord, complaining to Him that everything was going wrong and enumerating for Him a lengthy catalogue of catastrophe, to which the Lord replied, "That is the way I treat my friends." Teresa's rejoinder was, "Yes, Lord, that is why you have so few of them." This impertinence is not confined to Christians. The Persian poet Omar Khayyam, in the Moslem tradition (which has the Garden of Eden story in common with us), indicates in the quatrain below from the *Rubaiyat* that the Almighty needs to be forgiven by us as well as to accept our repentance.

Oh, Thou, who man of baser Earth didst make,
And ev'n with Paradise devise the snake:
For all the sin wherewith the Face of Man
Is blackened—man's forgiveness give—and take![1]

As a matter of fact, the whole of the *Rubaiyat* is as fine a bit of impertinence as there is in the literature of man.

But we should not think of Job as a petulant crybaby, shaking his fist at the Lord. He cannot capitulate to the urging of his friends, to admit guilt where he sees none. Moreover, if he does see and admit his guilt, how

---
[1] Omar Khayyam, *Rubaiyat* (New York, Random House, 1947) Rubaiyat, p. 100.

can God pardon him?
> If I think, 'I will forget my griefs,
> I will show a cheerful face and smile,'
>
> I tremble in every nerve;
> I know that thou wilt not hold me innocent.
>
> If I am to be accounted guilty,
> why do I labour in vain?
>
> Though I wash myself with soap
> or cleanse my hands with lye,
>
> thou wilt thrust me into the mud
> and my clothes will make me loathesome.
> (Job 9:27-31 NEB)

It is here that Job sees the necessity for a mediator, someone to stand between God and man and to bring them together. Job was expressing an implicit longing for the redeeming power experienced by Paul: "God was in Christ, reconciling the world unto himself" (2 Cor. 5:19 KJV).

But what was so clear to St. Paul by virtue of his acquaintance with Christ, is also seen in a rudimentary way by Job.

> He is not a man as I am, that I can answer him or that we can confront one another in court. If only there were one to arbitrate between us and impose his authority on us both,
>
> so that God might take his rod from my back, and terror of him might not come on me suddenly.
>
> I would then speak without fear of him;
> for I know I am not what I am thought to be.
> (Job 9:32-35 NEB)

One wonders whether that train of thought begun

here and elsewhere in the book of Job didn't inspire the unknown author called Second Isaiah* to describe this arbitrator in what are called the *suffering servant* pasages, some of which are quoted below:

Surely he hath borne our griefs,
and carried our sorrows:
yet we did esteem him stricken, smitten of God,
    and afflicted.

But he was wounded for our transgressions,
he was bruised for our iniquities:
the chastisement of our peace was upon him;
and with his stripes we are healed.

All we like sheep have gone astray;
we have turned every one to his own way;
and the Lord hath laid on him the iniquity of us all.
                                   (Isa. 53:4-6 KJV)

But Job has an even clearer vision of the one who is to save him. Unfortunately the passage is in some parts quite garbled in the Hebrew, and the hope of Resurrection, which the King James translators read into it, is not justified by the fragmentary Hebrew we have. Yet the older translation is couched in language more familiar to our theological expression so I will include the King James Version and a modern reconstruction for you to compare.

Oh that my words were now written!
oh that they were printed in a book!

That they were graven with an iron pen

---

*The book of the prophet Isaiah is divided into two distinct sections, the first part written by Isaiah of Jerusalem ends at the 39th chapter, and the balance was written in Babylon almost 200 years later by an unknown author known as Deutero-Isaiah. However, the earliest possible date for Job would be the sixth century which would put him only slightly earlier than second Isaiah.

and lead in the rock forever!

For I know that my redeemer liveth,
and that he shall stand at the latter day upon the earth:

And though after my skin worms destroy this body, yet in my flesh shall I see God:

Whom I shall see for myself, and mine eyes shall behold, and not another. . . . (Job 19:23-27 KJV)

O that my words might be inscribed,
O that they might be engraved in an inscription,

cut with an iron tool and filled with lead
to be a witness in hard rock!

But in my heart I know that my vindicator lives
and that he will rise last to speak in court;

and I shall discern my witness standing at my side
and see my defending counsel, even God himself,

whom I shall see with my own eyes,
I myself and no other. (Job 19:23-27 NEB)

Notice that Job sees the vindicator, not only as another person appearing in court on his behalf, but also as God himself. It is certain that this poet wrote better than he knew, and that, in a sense, he perceived the necessity for an incarnate Son of God without being aware of it.

Job ceases to give long discourses at the end of the 31st chapter, defiant to the end.

Let me but call a witness in my defence!
Let the Almighty state his case against me!
If my accuser had written out his indictment,
I would not keep silence and remain indoors.

No! I would flaunt it on my shoulder

and wear it like a crown on my head;

I would plead the whole record of my life
and present that in court as my defence.
>   Job's speeches are finished.
>   (Job 31:35-37 NEB)

The speeches of Elihu intervene, without adding much to the whole, and in some ways, interrupting the pace of the poem. If we move directly from the passage above to the 38th chapter we probably have the book as it was originally written.

As God speaks from the whirlwind, the puny demand of Job, (Let the Almighty state his case against me!) is lost in the overpowering succession of questions from God himself.

Then the Lord answered Job out of the tempest:

Who is this whose ignorant words
cloud my design in darkness?

Brace yourself and stand up like a man;
I will ask questions, and you shall answer.

Where were you when I laid the earth's foundations?
Tell me, if you know and understand.

Who settled its dimensions? Surely you should know.
Who stretched his measuring-line over it?

On what do its supporting pillars rest?
Who set its corner-stone in place,

When the morning stars sang together
and all the sons of God shouted aloud?
>   (Job 38:1-7 NEB)

And it goes on and on, this outpouring of questions, one less answerable than the last until finally, at the beginning of chapter 40:

Then the Lord said to Job:

Is it for a man who disputes with the
   Almighty to be stubborn?

Should he that argues with God answer back?

And Job answered the Lord:

What reply can I give thee, I who carry no weight?

I put my finger to my lips.

I have spoken once and now will not answer again:
twice have I spoken, and I will do so no more.
(Job 40:1-5 NEB)

   And then the Almighty goes on with his humiliating questioning for still two more chapters. And there, as in every utterance of God, is opportunity to rebel further, for God has not given Job a philosophical justification for the existence of evil or in any way helped to alleviate his pain or sense of the unjustice done him. And Job might have gone on, shouting ineffectual invective to the skies, but for two things that occurred to him. First, Job recognized, in the whirlwind, that God cared about him, cared enough to manifest himself to him, to describe to him the manifold ways in which His grace comes. And second, Job realized that this grace is sufficient for him, that he can put his faith in it, so he said:

I know that thou canst do all things
and that no purpose is beyond thee.

But I have spoken of great things
which I have not understood,
things too wonderful for me to know.

I knew of thee then only by report
but now I see thee with my own eyes.

Therefore I melt away;
I repent in dust and ashes.

(Job 42:2-6 NEB)

Discussion Guide

Much was made in this discussion of Job 7:11-21. Many men and women have had the sense of being pursued by God. Have you ever felt this way? Sometimes it seems this way when for some reason our conscience won't quit. But I am thinking more of God's calling us to a task or a particular way of life. Frances Thompson's poem, "The Hound of Heaven," is a modern example. Below is an ancient one.

Lord, you have searched me out and known me;
    you know my sitting down and my rising up;
    you discern my thoughts from afar.

You trace my journeys and my resting-places
    and are acquainted with all my ways.

Indeed, there is not a word on my lips;
    but you, O Lord, know it altogether.

You press upon me behind and before
    and lay your hand upon me.

Such knowledge is too wonderful for me;
    it is so high that I cannot attain to it.

Where can I go then from your Spirit?
    where can I flee from your presence?

If I climb up to heaven, you are there;
    if I make the grave my bed, you are there also.

If I take the wings of the morning
    and dwell in the uttermost parts of the sea.

Even there your hand will lead me
    and your right hand hold me fast.

If I say, "Surely the darkness will cover me,
and the light around me turn to night,"

Darkness is not dark to you;
the night is as bright as the day;
darkness and light to you are both alike.

For you yourself created my inmost parts;
you knit me together in my mother's womb.

I will thank you because I am marvelously made;
your works are wonderful, and I know it well.

My body was not hidden from you,
while I was being made in secret
and woven in the depths of the earth.

Your eyes beheld my limbs, yet unfinished in the womb;
all of them were written in your book;
they were fashioned day by day,
when as yet there was none of them.

How deep I find your thoughts, O God!
how great is the sum of them!

If I were to count them, they would be more in number than the sand;
to count them all, my life span would need to be like yours.

(Ps. 139:1-17 PBCP)

What is the attitude of the Psalmist toward God? How does it differ from Job's? Which writing best expresses your feelings? Do you sometimes feel one way and then the other? I do.

8

Everyman and the Fall

It must be remembered that the Bible is a library; that it contains books of theology, law, history, poetry, legends, drama and myths. Many people bristle when one uses the word myth in connection with the Bible, believing that the truth of the Bible is being attacked.

This chapter defines myth carefully as a vehicle of truth and discusses the most profound truth God has revealed concerning man. We must remember that biblical fundamentalism, as we know it today, is just over a hundred years old, a direct reaction to Darwinism. But as important in this chapter is the truth it conveys, a reality about man that has always existed, a reality that reveals in an unmistakable way our need for redemption and points to our redeemer.

This truth, revealed in the third chapter of Genesis, is reiterated on almost every page of the Bible, together with accounts of the various ways God is able to redeem evil and bring good from it.

Many lay persons who have just a casual acquaintance with the Bible seem to have the impression that the whole book is composed of factual history, or at least what purports to be factual. This impression seems to have been created by the kind of Sunday school program many of us knew as we were growing up.

I am sure many of those who taught my generation believed, for example, when they told us of the exploits of Samson that they were dealing with a historical personage, whereas, in reality Samson belongs in the category of legendary folk heroes like Beowulf, Paul Bunyan and his blue ox, Babe, and Pecos Bill.

The problem with such teaching is that it usually is the last the ordinary layman gets, and as he grows in sophistication himself, he comes to doubt some of the material that was taught to him as, dare I say, gospel, and usually in his college years, he rejects the whole of the Bible as being unworthy of his consideration. If he returns to the church at all, it is often when his oldest child reaches church school age and the process begins all over again. The tragedy of this is that much of the real wealth and richness of the Bible comes as a result of understanding the type of material being read and what it is trying to convey.

Among the various literary forms in the Bible, the myth is quite prominent. A myth is not a lie, or something false, but a profound truth too fragile for direct exposition, which is told in the form of a story. Not only are myths created by ancient and anonymous writers, but often myths are consciously produced by writers of prominence and stature. For example, Plato in the *Timaeus*, comes to a point where he simply cannot proceed with direct, expository writing, and in order to convey what he must, he invents the myth of the cave. Our Lord used a form of myth over and over in what we call parables. There was no prodigal son or good Samaritan in factual history, but the truths conveyed by this conscious device of inventing a story are unforgettable.

All of this is designed to introduce one of the most profound myths of all time, the account found in the third chapter of the book of Genesis which is commonly known as the Fall. This myth is the finest example of the editorial work of J, who took a very old myth and reworked it, changing its meaning and giving it the profound insight into the nature of man it now possesses. It is very difficult to reconstruct the earlier myth, but it might have gone something like this.

Man and woman lived in the garden, under the care of one of the gods. A rival god, in the guise of a serpent, caused the man and the woman to eat of the forbidden tree, which gave them power to challenge the god of the garden. The god then, fearing that they would also eat of the tree of life and become a further threat to him by being made immortal, expelled them from the garden. Let me carefully label this as conjecture. While there is some reasoning behind my reconstruction, other conjectures can also be made. The point is that the religion behind the early myths is primitive and polytheistic, and quite probably dualistic. (Dualism in religion is the concept that there are rival forces of good and evil, locked in a cosmic struggle that is always a draw.) The god of the garden is jealous of his power, which is maintained by magic trees producing magic fruit, the power of which he is unable to control except by denying access to the trees. In its original form it is a very ordinary myth indeed, like many dozens that can be found in folk literature.

But what a transformation this naive, primitive myth undergoes at the hand of J. The man is not simply a man or even the first man, but *adham*, which can be understood as a generic term for mankind, or more importantly, because of its implication for each of us, "Everyman," as I have it in the title of this chapter. The name Eve probably survives from the earlier myth but is quite appropriate to be used with Adam because of the implications of motherhood connected with it. Also, the god of the garden is not some minor league deity, fearful of losing his power, but Jahweh, the only God, the all powerful, who breathed the breath of life into man and made him a living soul. Even the serpent is no longer a competing deity but a creature of Jahweh, who wills to use his subtlety in contention against the Almighty, even though he owes his very existence to Him.

And so we have an entirely new cast of characters. God Almighty has placed Everyman and the Mother of All in a beautiful garden (perhaps creation itself) with all its fruit available except that from the one tree in the midst of it.

> The serpent was more crafty than any wild creature that the Lord God had made. He said to the woman, 'Is it true that God has forbidden you to eat from any tree in the garden?'
>
> The woman answered the serpent, 'We may eat the fruit of any tree in the garden except for the tree in the middle of the garden; God has forbidden us either to eat or to touch the fruit of that; if we do, we shall die.'
>
> The serpent said, 'Of course you will not die. God knows that as soon as you eat it, your eyes will be opened and you will be like gods knowing both good and evil.'
>
> (Gen. 3:1-5 NEB)

All the tempter ever needs to do is to get things moving, so that we begin to consider within ourselves the advisability of sinning. Once this began in Eve, all the serpent needed to do was to slither away and watch the fun.

We can believe that there is some space of time after

the serpent's statement, long enough for Eve to hunt up the tree and take a good look at it. We can be sure that this is what she would do, even if she had to walk the whole width of the garden to see it, so thoroughly had she been aroused. Upon inspection she found that it was indeed good for food, and moreover that it was pleasant to the eyes. It had not only appealed to her appetite but also to her aesthetic sense. And then she came up with the clincher. It was a tree to be desired to make one wise. She would then know. So she took. She ate.

Each person reading these words has only to remember some occasion of temptation to see the universality of this progression into sin. Vivid in my own mind is the trip behind the barn to experiment with tobacco. It went something like this.

TEMPTER: (in the form of an older contemporary) Do your folks *really* let you do anything you want to like you say?

I: Oh, sure they do. (afterthought) Of course they don't want me to do anything like smoking, because they say it will stunt my growth.

TEMPTER: (pulling out a pack of cigarettes in a very superior manner) It ain't gonna stunt your growth. I been smokin' for a long time and I'm big for my age. But if you don't want to, maybe I'd better wait till later. (Ostentatiously puts the pack away.)

I: Oh, go ahead! Let me see you do it.

And we all know what happened. He looked so nonchalant as he blew out the smoke, and as it wafted toward me it smelled so good that I realized that if I tried it I would know whether it tasted as good as it smelled. So thirty seconds later I was coughing away.

While the example above is quite trivial, it will serve to indicate that temptation, even to what may be inconsequential, follows a universal pattern. Moreover, no human being alive, or who has ever lived, has avoided the temptation to disobey the authority duly and rightfully constituted over him. This is, in its simplest form, a statement of the doctrine of original sin. This doctrine, derived from the myth we have been examining, while never popular, has fallen into real disfavor in our day. On a commonplace level, the objections are trivial and often sentimental.

"Do you mean to tell me that this sweet babe in his cradle is stained and tainted with sin?"

Yes, madam, I do, and the first time he blows Pablum in your face when you are trying to feed him, you will know what I mean.

While I think that J believed he was revealing a characteristic of all men, rather than writing about a particular man and woman in history, Adam and Eve have been considered to be historical personages by most of the readers of the account through the centuries. Earlier, the question of the historicity of the account was irrelevant, because the application of the process was seen to be universal. St. Augustine, for example, undoubtedly looked upon Adam and Eve as persons in history. At the same time, he identified himself as having lived through and reenacted this process of temptation and sin in his own life, and he knew, as well as any man who ever lived that the story of Adam and Eve is the story of every man and every woman.

But as we have grown in sophistication, particularly in biology, indeed in all of the natural sciences, we have come to the point when we need to discover the mythological origin of the doctrine of original sin. What is being expounded theologically is that we are somehow flawed, so that even our best efforts miss the mark because in making them, we always manage to exploit our own self interest, or to mix our motives. As theologians we do not talk of heredity or environment as the transmitter of original sin, but simply try to describe accurately the evidence that this universal penchant for disobedience is somehow transmitted.

We have not, however, exhausted the insights to be found in this myth. We cannot hope to do that, but there are other obvious points to be made. One is the knowledge that we all have through experience: that if we are at fault we try to find someone else to blame. We have the classic example of this phenomenon in Adam's statement: "The woman *whom thou gavest to be with me*, she gave me of the tree, and I did eat" (Gen. 3:12 KJV emphasis mine). You see, God, if you had just left well enough alone and not made that woman to be my helpmeet, then she wouldn't have existed to give me the forbidden fruit and it never would have happened. It's all your fault, God.

Further, there is the shame at the discovery by Adam and Eve that they were naked. A lot has been read into this that does not belong. Many believed in times past and even into the present, that the eating of the forbidden fruit in reality referred to engaging in the sex act by Adam and Eve, an act forbidden by God and therefore inherently evil.

But no one who knows the writing of the Jahwist could ever accuse him of thinking that. He believed that sex, among all other of God's creations, was good. But he also was fully aware of man's capacity to take any of God's good creations and to corrupt their goodness by using them exploitively, inappropriately, untimely, or to excess. And the Jahwist knew perfectly well that shame from being naked came not from some evil inherent in sex, but from the evil ways men look upon it, with its opportunities to make a travesty of relationship. The guilt comes from what man has taught himself to think about it rather than from the thing itself.

Finally, the expulsion from the Garden of Eden gives us an interesting clue about the Jahwist. He betrays to us the hard, demanding, agricultural environment from which he springs, in his account of God cursing the ground for Adam's sake. He writes with real feeling and we can assume first-hand information about the thorns and thistles the earth brings forth and the sweat of the face with which man eats his bread. Perhaps even more characteristic of this environment is the consignment of Adam to return to the dust from which he came, after having toiled in it his whole life.

It should be mentioned here that the Church does not believe that man suffers death because of his disobedience to God, but rather that the guilt resulting from the disobedience makes death a fearful, agonizing experience. Any experienced clergyman has seen many people die. In my experience, it is in the last moments of life when the returns are finally in and one can often see the effects of the redeeming grace of Christ. Many good pagans face death with resignation and fortitude, and many poor Christians face it in a kind of whimpering terror, but to me there is nothing more beautiful than the confidence and anticipation with which a faithful Christian embraces death.

It may be wondered why I chose one of the earliest parts of the Old Testament both in location in the book and in order of composition to close my discussion of that part of the Bible. The reason is that the myth of the Fall describes the need of every man for redemption. The rest of these thirty-nine books that comprise the Old Testament point up and reemphasize, in one way or another, that basic need. I have only sketched a few of these in this part of my book; indeed, I have left the very best parts for you to discover. As you do so, you will see how the myth of the Fall is applied over and over again to the situations in which the nation, Israel, as well as individuals in it, find themselves.

I hope you have followed some of these accounts I have written by looking up the references in the Bible itself and have found that they speak to you. I hope you will arm yourself with some good tools for further study; a Bible dictionary and a commentary that you find understandable and interesting. Then set about to read a little at a time and to think a lot about it. You notice how I have, in some cases, told the Bible account of an incident and then have rephrased it, with the help of my imagination, to fit a modern situation. You should take time to do these imaginings for yourself in your Bible reading, and when you master the technique you can do it far better than anyone can do it for you.

So I wish you well. I wish the joy of discovering for yourself the power of Amos's cry for justice, the wisdom of Isaiah of Jerusalem, the rugged persistence of Jeremiah, the poignant beauty of Lamentations, the sensitivity of Deutero-Isaiah, the drive of Ezekiel, and the splendid fantasy of Daniel. I hope as you read the Psalms they will sing in your head, for they are songs, songs for all moods and occasions. May you appreciate the pithiness of the Proverbs, understand and sympathize if not in some way identify, with the tired resignation of the author of Ecclesiastes, to thrill to the tenderness of the Song of Solomon. And there is so much more, hidden away in unlikely places.

But even so the Old Testament is an incomplete book. It is an account of needs stated, promises made but not fulfilled, a hopeful anticipation of something left to come. What is left incomplete in the Old Testament is fulfilled in the New.

Discussion Guide

If this chapter has been clear, you should be able to think of at least one clear parallel of the steps of temptation and sin from your own experience. How do you view temptation? In my theological terms, temptation results from one of God's fallen angels giving you very bad advice. Can you think of modern mythologies that deal with temptation? How about the gospel according to Sigmund Freud?

Below is what is an etiological legend, which is to explain the origin of something, in this case, the beginnings of different languages. Like many legends, it has very naive elements but also contains a profound truth.

> Once upon a time all the world spoke a single language and used the same words.
>
> As men journeyed in the east, they came upon a plain in the land of Shinar and settled there.
>
> They said to one another, 'Come, let us make bricks and bake them hard'; they used bricks for stone and bitumen for mortar.
>
> 'Come,' they said, 'let us build ourselves a city and a tower with its top in the heavens, and make a name for ourselves; or we shall be dispersed all over the earth.'
>
> Then the Lord came down to see the city and tower which mortal men had built, and he said, 'Here they are, one people with a single language, and now they have started to do this; henceforward

nothing they have a mind to do will be beyond their reach.

Come, let us go down there and confuse their speech, so that they will not understand what they say to one another.'

So the Lord dispersed them from there all over the earth, and they left off building the city.

That is why it is called Babel, because the Lord there made a babble of the language of all the world; from that place the Lord scattered men all over the face of the earth.

(Gen. 11:1-9 NEB)

How does this legend relate to the myth of the Fall? Does it reveal the same inclination to act without reference to God? To try to achieve heaven by human effort? Think about problems of communication today within various scientific and academic disciplines. How does this modern day Babel effect, for example, our dealing with problems of conservation and environment?

9

Jew and Greek

In spite of the attractiveness of the Canaanite fertility cults, the influence of the Egyptians, and the austerity of their own religion, the Jewish faith emerged after 1800 years of alien influence with religious connections strong and pure. A people who conceived of themselves to be a people favored in their history by Jahweh's intervention saw Jerusalem reduced to rubble by the Babylonians, and in captivity they became the people of the Book. At the time of Christ this Jewish culture was firm, resistant to outside influences, unique among peoples of the ancient world.

About the same time the dreaded sea people who were such a scourge to Egypt developed a unique culture of the Aegean peninsula, a culture continually asking questions about nature, man and God. This, too, became a highly developed culture, which by conquest overran the known world, and in the second century B.C. engaged in head to head conflict with the Jews in the Holy Land. This conflict of Jew and Greek produced no change in either. It remained for the Christ event to be the catalytic agent which combined with these two strong-willed cultures to form a third, unlike either and stronger than both, the culture and religion we know as Christian.

In the first chapter I said this: "The Hebrew lacked inclination, if not vocabulary, to say, 'I have an idea.' Rather, he would say, 'The angel of the Lord came unto me and he said . . .' by which he meant the same thing." Perhaps I should have said, "by which he described the same phenomenon." Here in this simple statement we have epitomized the struggle between Jew and Greek, between the Hellenic and the Syriac cultures. Superficially we are Greek in the way we ordinarily live our lives, and are much more inclined to say, "I have an idea," particularly in day-to-day situations, but the closer we come to those things of ultimate meaning, the more likely we are to attribute to God the streaks of light He sends us. So the struggle between the Hellenic and the Syriac goes on in us today.

There are some who say that the Philistines of the Old Testament are off-shoots of the ancient Minoan culture of the Island of Crete. If this is so, it is altogether possible that the combat between David and Goliath might well have been one of the opening encounters within this struggle which still, in a sense, continues in us.* This conflict had its manifestation on some of the great battle arenas of all time.

Every school boy knows of Marathon, Salamis and Thermopylae, though strictly from the Greek point of view which sees them as victories which saved Western civilization. From the Persian point of view, their conquering armies stopped because they had already conquered the rich and culturally productive Ionia on the eastern shore of the Aegean Sea and were willing to forego the conquest of the rocky, barren Aegean Peninsula as not being worth the trouble. It was in this

---

*I am indebted for this and for much that follows in this chapter to Dom Gregory Dix *JEW AND GREEK* Harper & Brothers, New York. For the title, however, we are both indebted to St. Paul. (Gal. 3:28).

forbidding land, however, that the Greeks, in the space of a century, got it all together, and created the civilization that still leaves its profound influence on the ways our minds work today.

The basic difference in these two cultures stems from their religious thought. The living God of the Old Testament, the one, almighty God who in the beginning created all things is the God who dominates the Syriac culture. It is most significant that of the five dominant religions of the world, three come from the Near East: Judaism, Christianity and Islam. These theistic religions see God as outside His creation, as the author of it and ruler over it. It is His will that directs it and will ultimately triumph; although He gives man freedom, and does not compel him to obey, He holds him responsible for the misuse of his freedom. Perhaps even more important is the concept that this living God is a God of history who acts in the lives of men.

In contrast, the Greeks saw the One as God and could go no further. Their God was detached from the cosmos, the universe, unknowable and unattainable. All attempts to explain the meaning of the world and of life were made by looking at the world itself rather than by coming to know the author of it. (Indeed, the Greeks looked upon such a relationship as an impossibility.) In Greek mythology, human history was the product of the three fates, the one who spun the thread of history, twisting into it the various strands of events, the second who measured out the thread, and the third who chopped it off. In other words, human history was capricious and incomprehensible.

Another way of making the distinction is to refer to the theistic religious as an open system in which God may intervene in innumerable ways: in theophany (a personal appearance in some way, as to Moses in the burning bush), by inspiration, by prophecy, by miracles, in any way He wants to. The Greek concept was that of a closed system in which everything that happened must be explained from within the system itself. From this distinction it takes little imagination to see that in the Syriac culture, worship and prayer are natural responses, whereas with the Greeks such exercises seem futile.

Into the very midst of this clash, "when the time was fully come" (Gal. 4:4), Jesus of Nazareth came into the world. He was born into the religious system of the Syrian and the political system of the Greek. He lived on the dividing line between the two worlds and the proximate cause of His death was the enmity between them. In the religion which grew up around His person, Jew and Greek traditions flowed together, supplemented and expanded each other, and created not a fusion or a synthesis of the two existing cultures, but a third, the sum indeed greater than its parts, which we know as Christianity. The beginnings of this development are recorded in the New Testament. They are the records, not of impartial observation with historical detachments, but of those who followed Jesus of Nazareth in the faith that He was indeed the long awaited Messiah. Just as the Exodus event formed the nation, Israel, and colored the whole of its thought, faith, and history, so the Christ event formed a New Israel, continuous with the old, proclaiming a gospel of salvation. The faith that grew out of this event has done more to influence the course of human history than any other factor we know.

Because the writers of the New Testament were committed to proclaiming the good news rather than to writing complete, accurate, and objective history, it is hard to know in their writings where the Jesus of history leaves off and the Jesus of faith begins. Yet the faith that God had indeed visited His people and had acted in a specific human life in a particular moment in time is at the core of the gospel proclaimed.

What is important is that they believed in that to which they bore witness, believed to the extent that the ordinary Greek word for witness, *martyr*, gained a new meaning. This ultimate witness they bore triumphantly and willingly, as men eagerly anticipating reunion with their risen and living Lord. If we cannot penetrate with accuracy behind this faith and cannot definitively separate the matters of history from it, we can share in the relationship with the Lord these early Christians worshiped.

In order to attempt to make the New Testament a little more understandable, some clergymen teach their congregations theories about how its passages can be scrutinized. Among them there has developed in the last fifty years a technique for examining the writing of the New Testament called "Form Criticism," which, while it is quite inexact and notoriously changeable as applied by different proponents of the theory, does furnish us with some tools for separating the actual words, deeds and thoughts of Jesus from the additions to or slanting of these by the community who were constituted by their faith that Jesus was the Messiah. The source of the revelation in either case is God, whether in the person of God the Son or God the Holy Spirit.

How does form criticism work? Bear in mind that while the Crucifixion must have taken place sometime between 29 and 33 A.D., the earliest writing of the New Testament, the epistles of Saint Paul began to appear about 49 A.D. and the earliest of the Gospels, Saint Mark, was probably written around 70 A.D. This means that there was a forty-year period before a serious attempt was made to record in a permanent way an account of the words and deeds of Jesus. Prior to the

Gospel according to Saint Mark, the traditions were verbal, probably, although there might have been a collection of sayings of Jesus, now lost, called Q (German Quelle, source), which supplied both Matthew and Luke with some of their material. Remember the discussion in the first chapter about oral tradition and the joke? Actually, the joke fits the definition of a folk form which gives the form critics their name. The original or basic part of a joke is the punch line which is really what it is meant to convey, and the framework, plain or elaborate, is of secondary importance. In a similar way, a form called *pronouncement stories* is common in the first three Gospels. Below is a good example:

A number of Pharisees and men of Herod's party were sent to trap him with a question. They came and said, 'Master, you are an honest man, we know, and truckle to no one, whoever he may be; you teach in all honesty the way of life that God requires. Are we or are we not permitted to pay taxes to the Roman Emperor? Shall we pay or not?' He saw how crafty their question was, and said, 'Why are you trying to catch me out? Fetch me a silver piece and let me look at it.' They brought one and he said to them, 'Whose head is this, and whose inscription?' 'Caesar's,' they replied. Then Jesus said, 'Pay Caesar what is due to Caesar, and pay God what is due to God.' And they heard him in astonishment.

(Mark 12:13-17 NEB)

The form critic would say that the original memory of Jesus is in the pronouncement, "Pay Caesar what is due to Caesar, and pay God what is due to God." The frame of the pronouncement might be a distorted reflection of what happened, or could possibly have been invented later by the Church, using Jesus' statement in a way that would seem to counsel a moderate attitude toward the Roman oppressors. However, Dom Gregory Dix comments on the same passage, saying that the framework is original and an essential part of the account. I have nowhere read Dom Gregory's opinions of form criticism, but since the conclusions he draws are almost always at variance with them, I imagine he puts little stock in their methods. If the theories of form criticism are helpful to you in clarifying the New Testament, they do no harm if you remember that God is the source of the Bible and all the words were set down by men through the power of the Holy Spirit.

A more useful example is in the parable of the sower, as found in Mark 4:3-20. In this parable there are two distinct parts, the first of which has the terse, provocative, telling style we associate with Jesus (vv. 3-9). The second half is a prosaic, longwinded and unimaginative explanation, which seems to have been added, no doubt, by some preacher.

Now look up the same parable in Matthew 13:3-23. Here, as is Matthew's custom, he has put into Jesus' mouth a lengthy quotation from Isaiah, showing the fulfillment of an ancient prophecy. Obviously, since the saying left the mouth of Jesus, a great deal has been added to it which fulfilled various needs for those who transmitted it.

I am not saying that this is bad. I am simply saying that there is no reliable way to separate what authentically comes from the mouth of Jesus or describes His actions and what grows out of the faith of the primitive church. It is said that a miracle would appear as a normal, commonplace event to someone casually looking at it. Yet for those to whom the event is a miracle, it is viewed as an extraordinary event with deep significance. To the Christian, the supreme miracle is the life, death, and Resurrection of Jesus Christ, revealing the Father to men on earth and reconciling them to Him. No one other than those who saw Jesus of Nazareth in this way has left any record of Him. And for me, the fact that He left as His legacy this believing, praying community which quite consciously calls itself His body on earth, is indication of the quality of His life and work which produced such a community.

This early Christian church was very thoroughly Jewish, not only ethnically, but in its thought as well. The Messiahship of Jesus was understood and proclaimed as the fulfillment of the promises made through the prophets by the living God of the Old Testament. There was no attempt to harmonize or explain the events, no doctrine of the Trinity or the Incarnation, simply the assertions that God is one, that the Father is God, that the Son is God, that the Holy Ghost is God, and that each differs from the other. Nor are these assertions direct, straightforward statements. Rather, they are ways of describing the way God acts that lead to these conclusions.

Here is a religious community, a sect of Judaism, which believes that it has a commission from its Lord to proclaim the gospel to the Greek-speaking world in which it finds itself. How can these basically Syriac religious concepts be made comprehensible to the Hellenic world? Obviously, there are great difficulties. There is the concept of the Messiah, which evolved and developed with its subtle overtones from the time of David. The Hebrew word means "God's anointed one" and refers to the custom of the anointing with oil of the Israelite kings by the prophets, indicating that they are God's chosen rulers. The closest these early Jewish Christians could come to an approximation of *Messiah* in Greek was *Christos*, which means, roughly, "smeared over with salve." Naturally, the real meaning of "Messiahship" escaped the Greek convert, who looked upon *Christos* as a surname of Jesus until he was deeply instructed in the faith.

But while there were differences which were enormous, there were also points of contact. The Old Testament had been translated into Greek and the word *Kyrios* (Lord) has been used extensively for God in that translation. Because of the polytheistic nature of Greek mythology, the word *Theos* (God) would have been misunderstood, but *Kyrios* conveyed to the Greek what the Hebrew meant by Jahweh. Moreover, *Word* had always been an important concept to the Hebrew, for example, as in God creating by the Word of His mouth. For the Greeks, *Logos* (Word) had come to mean the organizing principle of the world, and the connection between the two concepts had already been made in the wisdom literature of the Apocrypha and thoroughly Hellenized by a Jewish philosopher, Philo Judaeus, who was a contemporary of Jesus. It was a logical and meaningful step for Saint John to identify the *Logos* with God the Son, as he does in the prologue to his Gospel.

> When all things began, the Word already was.
> The Word dwelt with God, and what God was, the Word was.
>
> (John 1:1 NEB)

It is also possible for him to describe the Incarnation in the same prologue in a way comprehensible to both peoples:

> So the Word became flesh; he came to dwell among us, and we saw his glory, such as befits the Father's only Son, full of grace and truth.
>
> (John 1:14 NEB)

So the Jewish concepts behind the Gospels had undergone a process called Hellenization before they were ever written down in the form we have them. While many deplore this as a further barrier to understanding Jesus himself, it was a completely necessary development if Christianity was to survive and be known, a development that a Christian recognizes as part of the fabric of God's providence. Moreover, the questions raised by the Greeks concerning the meaning of existence are the basic questions of every man's life. The light that the Hellenized New Testament throws on these questions, therefore, has universal meaning.

So Jew and Greek meet in the New Testament, to proclaim a gospel which is neither Jewish nor Greek, though it borrows characteristics from both modes of thought. But the Christian gospel is a thing unique in itself. No one says this quite as well as Dom Gregory Dix in the closing lines of *Jew and Greek*:

'When the fulness of the time was come, God sent forth His Son, made of a woman, made under the Law, to redeem them that were under the Law, that we might receive the adoption of sons.'*
'In the fulness of time'—history can deal with that; the reckoning of time is part of its business. 'Made of a woman, made under the Law'—history can deal with that, too; the record of human life and the concrete particularities of it is a great part of its business. 'God sent forth His Son'—there history is helpless. That is from beyond history, which has no methods that can measure it. That is something which history can neither affirm nor deny. It can only ignore it or surrender to it. But it can still give evidence: it can tell us where the idea came from. The Greek looked around at the whole world and up to the whole sky, and said, 'The One is God'—and came to an impasse. But the Jew

---
*Gal. 4:4 seq.

looked back through history and said, 'God is one, and in the beginning He created the Heaven and earth'—and found that he could go forward from that in a Divine plan. 'To redeem them that were under the Law, that we might receive the adoption of sons.' The Gospel is no longer Jewish, but it was from the Jews.
—Dom Gregory Dix, *Jew and Greek*, pp. 111-112

Discussion Guide

Paul was a bridge person in the confrontation of Jew and Greek because he had superb training in Pharisaic Judaism, but also grew up in a Greek-speaking community, familiar with Greek learning. While he was phenomenally successful in developing Greek congregations, below is an incident of his failure.

Then Paul stood up before the Court of Areopagus and said: 'Men of Athens, I see that in everything that concerns religion you are uncommonly scrupulous.

For as I was going around looking at the objects of your worship, I noticed among other things an altar bearing the inscription "To an Unknown God." What you worship but do not know—this is what I now proclaim.

The God who created the world and everything in it, and who is Lord of heaven and earth, does not live in shrines made by men.

It is not because he lacks anything that he accepts service at men's hands, for he is himself the universal giver of life and breath and all else.

He created every race of men of one stock, to inhabit the whole earth's surface. He fixed the epochs of their history and the limits of their territory.

They were to seek God, and it might be, touch and

find him; though indeed he is not far from each one of us, for in him we live and move, in him we exist; as some of your own poets have said, "We are also his offspring."

As God's offspring, then, we ought not to suppose that the deity is like an image in gold or silver or stone, shaped by human craftsmanship and design.

As for the times of ignorance, God has overlooked them; but now he commands mankind, all men everywhere, to repent, because he has fixed the day on which he will have the world judged, and justly judged, by a man of his choosing; of this he has given assurance to all by raising him from the dead.'

When they heard about the raising of the dead, some scoffed; and others said, 'We will hear you on this subject some other time.'

And so Paul left the assembly. However, some men joined him and became believers, including Dionysius, a member of the Court of Areopagus; also a woman named Damaris, and others besides.
(Acts 17:22-34 NEB)

How do you account for the Athenians laughing at Paul? He was thrown in jail at Philippi, fought wild beasts at Ephesus, yet was successful. Most of his congregations grew out of conflict. What mistake did he make with the Athenians? Does Christian witness make similar error today?

10

Three Days in the Temple

The New Testament is a statement by persons who knew Jesus as Lord and testified to this faith. It is also, therefore, a statement of our faith that Jesus is Lord, that basis of our access to him as our Savior.

In this chapter we encounter the first instance in which Jesus demonstrates unique qualities of humanity, a humanity that differs from ours in degree rather than kind. Early on in the discussion Jesus is described as perfect man. We use the term "perfect" commonly in a different sense than it is used here. We think of perfection as without error like a 100 on a spelling paper or a ledger in balance. Perfection applying to Jesus' manhood means that he reached the full maturity or potentiality of his manhood, just as completely ripe fruit reaches the limit of its perfection. When we speak of Jesus in His human nature we speak of Him in this way, not as a hybrid half man—half God. When we speak of His divine nature it is a different story.

For those outside the Christian faith, the notion of the divinity of Jesus Christ is a great stumbling block. For those within it the humanity of Jesus Christ is often overlooked. Perhaps it is the emphasis of Christian teaching which tends to point up the divine in Christ and to play down His human side. Lurking, too, in the back of the Christian mind may be the notion that the temptations were not as real to Jesus as they are to us, because He was God; or that the suffering of the cross was easier to bear as a God-man than it would be for a man. Or perhaps it is that the relationship Christians establish in their life with Jesus is primarily a man-God relationship. But whatever the reason, for the committed Christian, it is the humanity of Jesus that is the source of wonderment.

Testimony to this difficulty is made by the well-known statue many devout Catholics display in their living rooms known as the *Infant of Prague*. It is a statuette of the infant Jesus in a kingly robe trimmed in ermine, an orb and sceptre in His hand. While it would be unfair to call the message proclaimed by this bit of sculpture a heresy, it is certainly accurate to say that it emphasizes one truth about the nature of Jesus at the expense of another. Certainly by the sixth century, when the Hellenizing of the Christian religion was complete, the dogma was, in its simplest form, that God the Son was one person with a divine and a human nature. However, the point of the humanity of Christ was not that He was only confined by the limits of His human nature when He wanted to be and that He called upon His divine power when He thought it was necessary; but rather, as perfect man, He realized the full potential of the humanity He shares with us. So when He was an infant He was like any other human infant who cried to make His needs known, who had to learn to talk and walk in the same way that we did. So the statue of the infant Jesus as ruler of the universe is at best, ridiculous, and at worst, a misleading distortion of truth. Yet, as the initial sentence of this paragraph suggests, the Infant of Prague witnesses to the difficulty we Christians find in accepting our Lord's complete humanity.

So if the child Jesus learned the things all human children learn, in the way they learn them, He learned to know the Father in the same way we learn to know Him. He had no special pipeline to God through which He received information and insight denied to any of us. The streaks of light flashed across His inner sight as they do with us, with the same fleeting vagueness. If this is not so, then He was not human at all. He learned to pray at His mother's knee, as we do. His was the conventional religious education of a pious peasant Jew of His day and nothing more.

Yet there was one substantial difference; one that belongs to a more efficient use of human qualities rather than the appropriation of divine ones. He was better at listening and obeying. Because He used all His faculties to hear the voice of God and the full force of His will to obey, the voice came clearer, and we may be quite sure, more demanding. But this opportunity is not denied to us. Indeed, because He listened and obeyed, the grace has been bought for us on the cross to do the same.

So it follows then that Jesus discovered His vocation from the Father in the way we discover ours. It is my conviction that God has a purpose for every man and reveals that purpose to all. We may not recognize the voice of God in our choice of what to do with our lives, but nonetheless, it is there. We may hear Him calling us through talents that we have, things that grab us and turn us on, skills we develop, or aspirations that grow within us. The more we are conscious that it is God who is calling and the more nearly we heed the call, the greater our fulfillment will be. You notice I said fulfillment, not satisfaction, or peace, or prosperity. Fulfillment may come through the damnedest struggle you can imagine, but because it is a struggle to which you are called, there is no fulfillment outside of it.

The first inkling of Jesus' consciousness of vocation is in the account of the three days He spent in the temple when He was twelve years old.

Now it was the practice of his parents to go to Jerusalem every year for the Passover festival; and when he was twelve, they made the pilgrimage as usual. When the festive season was over and they started for home, the boy Jesus stayed behind in Jerusalem. His parents did not know of this; but thinking that he was with the party, they journeyed on for a whole day, and only then did they begin looking for him among their friends and relations. As they could not find him they returned to Jerusalem to look for him; and after three days they found him sitting in the temple surrounded by the teachers, listening to them and putting questions; and all who heard him were amazed at his intelligence and at the answers he gave. His parents were astonished to see him there and his mother said to him, 'My son, why have you treated us like this? Your father and I have been searching for you in great anxiety.' 'What made you search?' he said. 'Did you not know I was bound to be in my Father's house?'

(Luke 2:41-49 NEB)

From the point of view of the form critics, this might be typical of the pronouncement story, in which case we should be solely concerned with the pronouncement, "Did you not know I was bound to be in my Father's house?", or, as the KJV has it, "Wist ye not that I must be about my Father's business?" For them, this would be the pronouncement probably uttered by Jesus sometime between His twelfth and twentieth year, under heaven knows what circumstances which had the framework of the pronouncement added to it to show what a precocious youngster He was. However, I am not so ready to throw out the framework of the account.

There is a theory that St. Luke, to whom we are indebted for this incident, was a careful historian who did quite a lot of original research with which he supplemented the material he found in Mark and got from Q. You remember Q as Quelle, the source now last used by Matthew and Luke. There is quite a lot of evidence in the book itself to support the idea that its author was a knowledgeable and sophisticated writer, acquainted with the Greek historian, Thucydices. Further, there is a tradition that he spent quite a lot of time in Jerusalem, interviewing those close to Jesus, among them His mother, Mary, or someone intimate with her. I doubt that this tradition would find much support among some of the New Testament scholars today, but the episode quoted above, if authentic, would have to come from Mary herself.

Certainly it is told from a woman's point of view. Notice, however, evidence of a much greater permissiveness than is characteristic of the American mom of the twentieth century. How many modern mothers, having journeyed from Cincinnati to Montreal to visit the Exposition with a group of friends and relatives, would return a day's travel on the trip home without checking to see if the child Jesus were not where she could keep a protective eye on him. However, men children grew up more quickly in those days, and with much less protection. Nevertheless, the mother's anxiety, perhaps intermingled with some guilt at being the least bit negligent even for that day and time, is expressed in a universal way. Can't you hear it from your childhood, expressed in the language of your day?

"Son, why did you do this to us? Your father and I have been worried sick about you."

It was always mother who said it and she said it just that way.

This has started me wondering about some of the pronouncements I made in response to that question. I can remember an early instance when this query was put. I was about six years old and walking home from school when I came upon a group of workmen who were digging up the stump of a large tree. In those days there were no chain saws or other mechnical aids, nothing but tedious, backbreaking labor. So I began my first tour of duty as a sidewalk superintendent, and I was not aware of the passage of time until my father and mother drove up, having sought me sorrowing. I am almost certain that I have recorded above verbatim what was said to me. And I can remember the gist of my reply.

"Gee, mom, I knew it was educational so I thought I had better stay and watch."

Certainly that was not a pronouncement in the league with: "Wist ye not that I must be about my Father's business?" But it did break mom and dad up and got me off the hook.

But I am not satisfied with the translation of Jesus' pronouncement in either of the versions I have quoted. The King James, beginning with "Wist ye not" is clearly archaic, but the rest of it does give a possible paraphrase of the Greek of the original. The New English Bible introduces a notion I can't find in the Greek, namely, "Didn't you know I was bound to be in my Father's house?" and we might paraphrase the following addition: "So why did you bother to look anywhere else?" I'm a little sorry the Greek doesn't support this idea, because I am sure it was close to what was in the mind of Jesus, and it expresses one of the universal characteristics of vocation, the quality of believing that because the impact of calling is so intense to you, everyone else must be aware of it also.

Either translation certainly reflects the feeling of the original. The nearest I can puzzle it out here in the woods with nothing but my rusty Greek and the Wescott and Hort version of St. Luke is this: "Had you not known that it is necessary for me to be in the things of my Father?"

Certainly this is not deathless English prose, but it is faithful to the Greek. I suppose the "things of my Father" could mean equally well "my Father's business" and "my Father's house." But it also means my Father's everything else, a total commitment to all that concerns the Father, which is all there is. That is quite a statement for a twelve-year-old.

One wonders how and when this sense of vocation began to develop. Certainly it did not begin in those three days in the temple, for there had to be quite a lot of background of interest, study, thought and meditation to prepare for the encounter and the impression it made. Even though there is a vivid experience of a call, as was true of Saint Paul, Saint Augustine or Martin Luther, there is an abundance of preparation before it. To develop the case of only one of these, Saint Paul was antagonistic to the infant Church and did his utmost to destroy it, simply because he couldn't get it out of his mind. We might conjecture that he saw something in the face of the dying Stephen that all the rigorism and pharisaism on which he had built his life could not produce for him. Perhaps this was the goad mentioned by Christ in the conversion experience of Paul, which prodded him onward despite his will to resist (Acts 26:14). Maybe, because of this resistance, he had to be struck blind in order to see the light.

We must believe that Jesus listened and obeyed from

the beginning if the author of the epistle to the Hebrews is correct when he says that Jesus ". . . was in all points tempted like as we are, yet without sin." We sin either in not hearing what we don't want to hear, or not obeying if what we hear does not suit us. For us the discovery of vocation is a business of fits and starts, but with Jesus it must have progressed smoothly and developed early. We can only conjecture about what might have gone on in the temple during those three days, but we can be sure there was content to it, for that is quite a block of time.

Clergymen today are subjected to many three day conferences and it is an exhausting process if there is something vital to talk about and boring if there is not. We can be sure that the doctors in the temple were not going to waste three days with childish prattle. We can imagine that Jesus began as the questioner but soon, because of the penetration of the queries He made, became the one questioned. It must have been an exhilarating experience for all concerned.

There is considerable evidence in the New Testament that Jesus had an exciting approach to Scripture. We can imagine it manifested in the scene in Nazareth when Jesus read for the first time in His home-town synagogue:

> The Spirit of the Lord God is upon me because the Lord has anointed me; he has sent me to bring good news to the humble, to bind up the broken-hearted, to proclaim liberty to captives and release to those in prison; to proclaim a year of the Lord's favour and a day of the vengeance of our God. (Isa. 61:1-2 NEB)

The New Testament tells of the hush that came over the congregation. I suppose it is always so when the local boy gives his first sermon in his home church.

The people pay attention at this point, if they never do again. Everyone is straining to hear what he does with this text, but no one is prepared for what comes forth: "This day is this scripture fulfilled in your ears" (Luke 4:21 KJV).

It is too bad we don't have the rest of what He said, but what a beginning! He lets them know not only that the Spirit is upon Him, presumption enough for a beginning preacher, but also that the things being prophesied are to be fulfilled in Him. No wonder they were amazed, for here is a frank, open confession of vocation. But, true to the definition of miracle given earlier, one man's miracle is another man's commonplace. There were those who said, "Isn't this the son of Joseph the carpenter? Who does he think he is?"

But we can well imagine that there were many times when He expounded the Scriptures that He caused the hearts of men to burn within them, as was true of those He met on the road to Emmaus after His Resurrection (Luke 24:32). Certainly the first men to have had this experience must have been the doctors in the temple during those three days.

Discussion Guide

We have discussed the faith of Israel as the expectation that God would communicate with the nation through their history—national and personal. In the New Testament we are confronted with Jesus as the embodiment of God's loving concern for us as our Savior. This demands a new dimension of faith on our part. The words of Jesus call us to new life in Him. His action on the cross shows them not to be mere words, but words He backs up with His own life. We cannot have Him and be content with our lives as they are. His call is to constant demand for change and growth, a shattering challenge to the status quo of life as we know it. But this is all reinforced by a promise.

> In truth, in very truth I tell you, he who has faith in me will do what I am doing; and he will do greater things still because I am going to the Father.
>
> Indeed anything you ask in my name I will do, so that the Father may be glorified in the Son.
>
> If you ask anything in my name I will do it.
> (John 14:12-14 NEB)

What is the nature of the power given us in this passage? What are the restrictions? Does the Church take much advantage of it? Do you? What is the element lacking which causes us to ignore this power?

11

What a Stranger Taught Our Lord

We have spoken repeatedly about meeting God in the Bible, but have not much emphasized the fact that we meet Him there as God the Holy Spirit. It is the Holy Spirit who not only, as the Nicene Creed states, "Spoke by the Prophets," but He also breathed the breath of life into the whole Bible. It is by the power of the Holy Spirit that the Bible was written, assembled, edited, and copied. Yet all of this was done through human agency, by those inspired by the Holy Spirit. When we encounter God on the pages of the Bible it is the Holy Spirit in us that brings it about.

We have emphasized that Jesus was perfectly human in His earthly life. Therefore, it is this same Holy Spirit that enabled Him to know the Father, to encounter Him in the scrolls of the Old Testament, and from time to time, through the mouths of other human beings. Therefore, to be strictly accurate perhaps I should have called this chapter "What the Holy Spirit Taught Our Lord Through the Mouth of a Stranger." But I want the assumption to be clear that the Holy Spirit can act through anyone He wants to act through and to teach anyone anything He wants taught. We accept this rather easily when it applies to persons we revere as being particularly holy, but we rebel at the notion that God might make an infidel His agent. And we certainly rebel against the idea that anyone could teach Jesus anything. The popular image seems to be that Jesus emerged from the womb of the Virgin with a knowledge of Sanskrit and Quantum Physics. Perhaps this chapter will demonstrate that the Holy Spirit spoke to Jesus through many mouths.

It is well known that after the Exodus the children of Israel made a conquest of the area we call the Holy Land and wrested it from a people called the Canaanites. What is less well known is that these Canaanite people were civilized and sophisticated far above their Israelite conquerors. The Canaanites were the forerunners of the people we know from our study of world history as the Phoenicians, to whom we are indebted for the alphabet, among other things.

In the course of the conquest by Israel of the Canaanites, and in subsequent centuries, there was a considerable intermingling of the religious ideas of Canaan with Jahwism, and then came periods of reform, when these alien elements were purged from the religion of Israel. The fertility worship of Canaan, with its temple prostitutes, both male and female, and its tractable gods who could be propitiated and bent to the will of the worshiper by the proper words and ceremonies, stood in strong contrast to the austere morality of the religion of Jahweh, the living, untamed God whose will dominated the lives of men. Certainly in periods of relative prosperity and calm these Canaanite deities were quite attractive to Israel. However, as the years went by and the Canaanite influence lessened, what was remembered by the Jews was the hatred and enmity toward Canaan. This antagonism continued even into New Testament times and was then directed toward the descendants of the Canaanites, the Syro-Phoenician neighbors of Israel to the north.

It was into the area where these people lived that our Lord, accompanied by His disciples, had ventured and had met the stranger who taught Jesus a lesson. The record of this encounter exists both in Mark 7:24-30 and in Matthew, and since Matthew's account contains all that is in Mark's and then some, I am using it as the basis of our discussion.

> Jesus then left that place and withdrew to the region of Tyre and Sidon. And a Canaanite woman from those parts came crying out, 'Sir! have pity on me, Son of David; my daughter is tormented by a devil.' But he said not a word in reply. His disciples came and urged him: 'Send her away; see how she comes shouting after us.' Jesus replied, 'I was sent to the lost sheep of the house of Israel, and to them alone.' But the woman came and fell at his feet and cried, 'Help me, sir.' To this Jesus replied, 'It is not right to take the children's bread and throw it to the dogs.' 'True, sir,' she answered; 'and yet the dogs eat the scraps that fall from their masters' table.' Hearing this Jesus replied, "Woman, what faith you have! Be it as you wish!' And from that moment her daughter was restored to health. (Matt. 15:21-28 NEB)

This passage raises a number of questions and I suppose the first one is: What was Jesus doing in the land of a hated and unclean people, (from His point of view) in the first place. A good conjecture would be, if we accept Mark's chronology, which is also reflected in Matthew, that the passages immediately preceding the part quoted record that Jesus had done a rather thorough job of taking on the religious establishment, and had probably made himself as popular as the dog in the neighbor's flower bed in that part of Galilee, so that He and His disciples had to leave for a while until things quieted down. Another theory is that they went into a desolate country among strange people who could be counted on, for the most part, to leave them alone and give them some badly needed respite from the press of the crowds. But for whatever reason, they had crossed the frontier and were in a strange land.

Another question is: in what language did the conversation take place? It is quite certain that neither Jesus or the disciples could understand the native language of this woman, nor could she understand the Aramaic that He spoke. So the language they both understood would be Greek. Mark calls her a Greek, which may be a memory of the tongue in which the encounter took place, whereas Matthew, who seems to have additional and corroborative information, makes her a native of Canaan. There are some who think Mark was a Roman who would have been unlikely to know the finer points of Middle Eastern geography and culture, while Matthew probably has it right.

The fact that Jesus and this foreign woman had a common language in which they could converse points to a significant reality of the first-century world, one that greatly aided to the spread of the Apostolic church. This was the phenomenon of being able to travel from what is now England to what is now India and being understood in Koine (common) Greek, which was an almost universal language of the time. This Koine Greek developed as the language of the military of the time of Alexander the Great, when Greek-speaking soldiers brought together a variety of dialects, and using the Attic Greek as a base, modifying it and simplifying it by the less complex inflections of the other dialects, forged a rough and ready tongue which was to be the almost universal language of the Greek and Roman world of the first and second centuries. It was the language of the streets, the marketplaces and bazaars, of the seaways and trade routes, and all but the most rustic and isolated peasants could converse in it. The more one studies the New Testament world, the greater the feeling is that God did indeed send His Son when the fullness of the time was come. Certainly the ease of communication afforded by a language that cut across ethnic boundaries would seem to be a mark of propitious timing.

So the conversation must have taken place in Greek. But the woman was not completely ignorant of the Jewish culture just south of the border, nor of the young wonder worker it had produced. However, one wonders what was in her mind as she addressed Him, "O Lord, thou Son of David." *Lord* certainly must not have carried for her any content of divinity, but simply was a polite form of addressing a person she felt to be her superior. The New English Bible translates it correctly as "Sir." Neither was "Son of David" likely to have had any Messianic connotations, but simply was an ethnic label, identifying Jesus as a Jew. But she had undoubtedly heard of the healing miracles He had performed, and it having been rumored that He was in her land, she sought him out on behalf of her daughter.

The response, in the form of what the poor woman could interpret only as a stony silence, seems to many Christians to be out of character in Jesus. This is due to the reluctance of the faithful to recognize and accept His humanity, as we indicated at some length in the last chapter. On the other hand, all of the training Jesus had received, all of the pronouncements of those in religious authority, and certainly the common folklore He grew up with emphasized the election of the Jews as God's chosen people and therefore His sole concern. In the face of such overwhelming pressure to make Him believe the contrary, it is not surprising to me that the human Jesus was not aware at that time that He was sent to redeem all men. While there are many voices to be found in the Old Testament to support the concept that Jahweh is the God of all nations, they are far from being the dominant voices. Moreover, Jesus lived at a time when the Jews were a conquered people but whose spirit was unbroken and whose sense of nationalism was never higher. This even increased the pressure on Him.

So it is not surprising that the first reply to the woman's entreaty was silence. But what did this silence mean? Jesus frequently used silence eloquently and appropriately. Certainly the correct response to the flippancy of Herod or the arrogance of Pilate was silence. When Peter had done denying Jesus, the silent look he got from the Master broke his heart so that he went out and wept bitterly. But that telling silence also brought about the beginning of Peter's redemption.

Here in the presence of this woman, Jesus may have used this silent moment to ask himself the question He had never before raised. What was his obligation toward the Gentiles? His thought was broken by the rude, unquestioning cry of the disciples:

'Send her away; see how she comes shouting after us.' (Matt. 15:23 NEB)

Their request turned His mind back to the familiar ground of His culture, so He said, as if to continue the argument that had been going on within himself silently:

'I was sent to the lost sheep of the house of Israel, and to them alone.' (Matt. 15:25 NEB)

At least she had gotten a response and a kindly one. So she was encouraged and persisted. The King James Version says that she worshiped Him, but that is a little stronger in English than the Greek implies. The New English Bible catches the flavor more nearly: "she came and fell at his feet." To believe that she thought in terms of attributing divinity to Him would carry one somewhat further than the language permits. However, she did have faith in His capacity to help her and she asked Him to do so.

Jesus was still wrestling with the problem. He had misgivings and didn't hesitate to express them in terms of the prejudice which had been programmed into Him.

'It is not right to take the children's bread and throw it to the dogs.' (Matt. 15:26 NEB)

He was thinking of the magnitude of His task, the enormous amounts of spiritual and psychic energy that He had been expending and would continue to expend. These are strictly human thoughts that are inextricably bound up with bodies that get tired and souls that agonize. They spring from the finitude of human nature. It is not surprising that they occurred to Jesus. Indeed, if they had not occurred we would have had to have denied His humanity.

The point of this whole chapter is that as God the Holy Spirit works through others sometimes to enlighten us, so God the Holy Spirit worked through the agency of a foreign woman of a despised race to teach our Lord the scope of his vocation. The Holy Spirit has indeed been given, as Jesus promised, to lead us into all truth, but He has been given to a community as well as to individuals, a community united by a common faith.

The delicacy of the reply of the Syro-Phoenician woman may be indicative of the source of her inspiration, for it is a combination of wit and humility that touched the heart of Jesus and convinced Him.

'True, sir,' she answered; 'and yet the dogs eat the scraps that fall from their masters' table.'

(Matt. 15:27 NEB)

In the mind of Christ, if I may presume to consider what was there, a barrier had been broken down and a vista had opened up. He found, in a way that all men learn, that He was indeed sent for the salvation of all peoples. It is in the true and complete humanity of Jesus that the wonder lies. One way I like to express the miracle of the Incarnation to myself is by thinking that the vision, the intent, the purpose God conceived in making man is embodied in the human life of Jesus Christ. Since God is eternal, within Him is no growth or development, ideas coming or going or mind changing. Therefore, the concept of mankind which Jesus embodied has always been in the mind of God. This is exactly what the creed means when it says that Christ was "begotten of His Father before all worlds." And wonder of wonders, this Incarnation did not take place in some prehistoric and legendary past, clouded by the mists of time, but in a period and at a place identifiable in human history, in a stable in Bethlehem during the reign of Caesar Augustus, when Cyrenius was governor of Syria. It is faith in this act of God intervening in the history of men to reveal himself by a Son that has changed and enriched the lives of millions of souls since that time. It is a faith that was caught by a strange woman in a strange land that opened the eyes of our Lord to the universal scope of His ministry and caused Him to exclaim:

O woman, great is thy faith: be it unto thee even as thou wilt.

Discussion Guide

I suppose there might only be two groups in the Holy

Land in our Lord's earthly life who might be more hated than the Syro-Phoenicians. Can you think who they might be? I believe the Samaritans would be one group and the Romans would be the other. Yet, in the story Jesus told of the Good Samaritan, Jesus, in making up the parable, does not reveal the Holy Spirit inspiring the actions of the respected priest or Levite, but the hated Samaritan. In the passage below the Holy Spirit reveals much to a Roman centurion. See if you can count the ways.

> When he had entered Capernaum a centurion came up to ask his help. 'Sir,' he said, 'a boy of mine lies at home paralysed and racked with pain.' Jesus said, 'I will come and cure him.' But the centurion replied, 'Sir, who am I to have you under my roof? You need only say the word and the boy will be cured. I know, for I am myself under orders, with soldiers under me. I say to one, "Go", and he goes; to another, "Come here", and he comes; and to my servant, "Do this," and he does it.' Jesus heard him with astonishment, and said to the people who were following him, 'I tell you this: nowhere, even in Israel, have I found such faith.
>
> Many, I tell you, will come from east and west to feast with Abraham, Isaac, and Jacob in the kingdom of Heaven. But those who were born to the kingdom will be driven out into the dark, the place of wailing and grinding of teeth.'
>
> Then Jesus said to the centurion, 'Go home now; because of your faith so let it be.' At that moment the boy recovered. (Matt. 8:5-13 NEB)

What did the Holy Spirit reveal to the centurion? How did the Holy Spirit prepare for the encounter between Jesus and the centurion? How did the centurion understand the authority of Jesus? Can you think of other places in the Bible where Jesus' unique authority is mentioned? How did the Spirit in Jesus respond?

12

Jesus, the Law and Grace

This is a chapter about the most glorious freedom a person can know. It is the freedom that comes when anger and resentment have been flushed out of us by forgiveness and we are able to love someone once again. It is the freedom we experience when God's absolving mercy washes away our sins and we are free from the nagging guilt of the past and are able to function in the God-given opportunities of the glorious present unhampered. It is the freedom we know when faith sponges away anxieties, and we see creative alternatives to what were formerly escape-proof traps. Jesus, throughout the Gospels, lives out this freedom in His actions and guides us to it with His words. By being drawn into the field of force generated by Jesus and thereby living in Christ, Saint Paul bears witness to his own deliverance from the paralyzing power of compulsive legalism to become a new man living in the Spirit.

All this is made possible through a mysterious and compelling quality we call grace. Through Jesus we know what it means and from Jesus it is made available to us. The Church has always been a means to this freedom, though at times she seemed to have kept it well hidden. She has held it close to the heart for centuries in the phrase, *Cui servire regnare,* so happily paraphrased by Thomas Cranmer, "Whose service is perfect freedom."

One of the most persistent pieces of misinformation about the Christian religion is that it is a religion of law. Many men in the pew, who ought to know better, believe that successful Christian living consists of obeying the Ten Commandments and the parts of the Sermon on on the Mount they can understand. Even worse, there are whole sects of Christianity who see all human sin to be tied to sex and alcohol. Within these are some of the most rigid, inflexible, and murderously angry persons I have ever known. It is out of this kind of misconception of the religious revolution wrought by Jesus that Sunday closing laws and other such bluenose legislation develop. A patent bit of hypocrisy which was much a part of the United States Navy during World War II, and which may still persist, was the announcement that used to come over the loudspeaker:

> Now hear this. Church call. Church call. The smoking lamp is out. Knock off all card games and loud talking throughout the ship.

The kind of joyless Christianity that produces notions that such an announcement is pleasing to the Almighty is as foreign to Jesus' thought as the popular Jewish concept prevalent in His day, that the Messiah would be a military leader who would break the yoke of the Roman conquerors.

In order to understand the attitude of Jesus toward the concept of law, we need to examine the religious framework into which He came. We have mentioned elsewhere the idea that God's law is woven into the very fabric of creation, to be discovered rather than legislated. Since in Judaism there is no distinction between religious law and secular law as there is with us, all of the additions, commentaries, interpretations, all the minutiae of subsequent legislation are also considered to be part of the divine law. So what had begun originally as the concept that God cared about the way men behave grew to such proportions that the law itself, in a way, became a god, and the worship of it a monstrous idolatry.

The sheer volume of legislation with the commentary and interpretation of it, both oral and written, was such that the mastery of it was the life work of a learned few. This tended to develop a kind of religious elite in Judaism, the scribes and lawyers working at it professionally, and the Pharisees, members of a party within the religion, insisting on the validity of the whole law, written and oral. While these groups were not identical, they were overlapping. Jesus pointed out that this preoccupation with the minutiae of law was occasion for two evils, one being the neglect of the weightier demands of the law—justice, mercy and good faith, (Matt. 23:23) and the other being the ostentatious way in which pious acts were done (Matt. 6:2-4). There are many more passages that illustrate such ideas but these two are quite clear. Even more important in Jesus' teaching was the emphasis on internal attitudes of mind in moral behavior rather than obedience to external codes of law. Symbolic of this concept is this phrase recorded by St. Mark:

> Listen to me, all of you, and understand this: nothing that goes into a man from outside can defile him; no, it is the things that come out of him that defile a man.
>
> (Mark 7:14-15 NEB)

Probably the most highly regarded moral and ethical teaching in the world's literature is found in the fifth, sixth and seventh chapters of the Gospel according to

St. Matthew, known commonly as the Sermon on the Mount. However, it is not a catalog of rules but a description of behavior. In almost every sentence one can sense the attitudes that make the behavior possible, and one also realizes that if the attitudes described were those of most men, the world would be infinitely changed for the better. But there is a nagging awareness that these are somehow above us, seemingly out of reach through the agency of our own strength and circumstance.

No one can really comment on the Sermon on the Mount for another. Each person who reads it brings his own background, his own morality and behavior to it, and the magnificent concepts contained therein work their magic on each in a unique way. But there are a few verses I would like to lift out for some observations.

> How blest are those who know their need of God;
> the kingdom of Heaven is theirs.
>
> How blest are the sorrowful;
> they shall find consolation.
>
> How blest are those of a gentle spirit;
> they shall have the earth for their possession.
>
> How blest are those who hunger and thirst to see right prevail;
> they shall be satisfied.
>
> How blest are those who show mercy;
> mercy shall be shown to them.
>
> How blest are those whose hearts are pure;
> they shall see God.
>
> How blest are the peacemakers;
> God shall call them his sons.
>
> (Matt. 5:3-9 NEB)

These are some of the famous Beatitudes. Notice that

each one quoted describes an attitude of mind which is ongoing and habitual. Contrast this with a legal system which tries to prescribe correct action for every conceivable situation. How could one ever develop a legal system which, if followed, would produce a gentle spirit or a peacemaker? So at the very outset Jesus is dealing with concepts that are not only different from those of the religious establishment but which are threatening to it. Not that the legal system doesn't try to achieve a high standard of moral behavior. For example:

> When you reap the harvest of your land, you shall not reap right into the edges of your field; neither shall you glean the loose ears of your crop; you shall not completely strip your vineyard nor glean the fallen grapes. You shall leave them for the poor and the alien. I am the Lord your God.
> (Lev. 19:9-10 NEB)

Contrast this with:
> How blest are those who show mercy;
>   mercy shall be shown to them.

In the first case, the legislator, by implication, takes upon himself the task of ultimately codifying each merciful act. In the second, the individual is responsible for developing an attitude which automatically produces merciful acts. Imagine how different these words of Jesus must have sounded to those who were accustomed to the expounding of legalists. No wonder they noted that Jesus spoke as one having authority, not as the scribes and Pharisees. They recognized that His teaching proceeded out of an inner source of power rather than from a group of loosely connected quotations from this or that authority. And that which Jesus had within himself He was concerned that each man develop. But Jesus was also quite conscious of what He was doing to legalistic concepts, so much so that He found it necessary, before He had gone very far in the sermon, to defend the law.

> Do not suppose that I have come to abolish the Law and the prophets; I did not come to abolish, but to complete. I tell you this: so long as heaven and earth endure, not a letter, not a stroke, will disappear from the Law until all that must happen has happened.
>
> (Matt. 5:17-18 NEB)

As suggested above, any codification of law is bound to be incomplete simply because it is impossible to imagine all that can possibly happen, and if it were possible to imagine it and set it down, no one could ever learn all he would need to know of such law. But in developing attitudes that produce tight behavior, the work of the law is completed. The New English Bible has an alternate reading to the last phrase quoted above, "before all it stands for has been achieved." The Greek behind this phrase cannot be translated literally because the Greek language does with tenses of verbs what we have to do by adding words and phrases. I believe the alternate reading more nearly catches the spirit of the Greek, although it is slightly further from the letter. Certainly what Jesus means is that the law will have to exist until the attitudes behind its provisions are fully and universally developed. St. Paul enlarges on this idea.

> Thus the law was a kind of tutor in charge of us until Christ should come, when we should be justified through faith; and now that faith has come, the tutor's charge is at an end.
>
> (Gal. 3:24-25 NEB)

One could multiply examples endlessly throughout the Sermon on the Mount of the distinctive way Jesus had of teaching moral concepts. But this would not add much that has not been already said, and I leave you to discover the examples on your own. However, before I turn to other things I want to share with you a bit of exegesis I learned from an alcoholic Danish carpenter in a bar, after he had just hocked his tools to buy everyone in the place a drink. The passage he was talking about is found in Matthew 7:3-5 and is almost incomprehensible in King James English, with its talk about motes and beams. This is the way his explanation went.

I don't know much about the Bible and I haven't read any of it since I left Denmark, but I always liked the part where it says you oughtn't to try to take the sliver out of your brother's eye until you remove the plank from your own.

This conversation took place ten years before the New English Bible came out, using "speck of sawdust" and "plank" in its translation of the passage in question. But the Danish carpenter, drunk or sober, has it beat. I guess it takes a carpenter to understand one.

But how do we develop these attitudes Jesus talks about? How do we get the frame of mind that enables us to turn the other cheek, to love our enemies, to rid our hearts of murderous anger, or to look at and appreciate a pretty girl without mentally climbing into bed with her? Surely one of these attitudes, at least one, gives you trouble. Something happened to those persons who knew, accepted and followed Jesus that eventually changed them internally. Peter changed from a blustering braggart coward to a person of great courage. John was a quick tempered, rebellious teenager, whom Jesus called Son of Thunder, but he became the apostle of love, whose ministry in his old age finally distilled itself into three words: "Love one another." In *Jesus Christ Superstar* Mary Magdalene says, "I've loved lots of men, but how do I love this man." The Gospels testify that she learned and it turned around her life.

These persons, and millions who have lived after them, have had one thing in common: faith in God through Jesus Christ. And as a result of that faith, their lives were changed internally. They thought differently and they acted differently. Somehow, as a result of this faith, they received power to do what they were powerless to do before. This power has a name. It is called grace, and it comes from God unmerited and unearned. It is free. I remember during my theological studies trying to fathom the meaning of grace. I sought meaning in it as a thing in itself. But I finally discovered that grace is grace to do something: to love the unlovable, to have patience when the capacity for it seems exhausted, to speak courageously when it would be much easier and safer to maintain a cowardly silence. Moreover, this grace does not come because you strive for it, for there is no way you can do so. It comes from God and brings with it the harvest of the Spirit.

> But the harvest of the Spirit is love, joy, peace, patience, kindness, goodness, fidelity, gentleness and self-control. There is no law dealing with such things as these.
>
> (Gal. 5:22-23 NEB)

No one can gain any of these qualities by gritting his teeth and saying that he will. You can't, with firm resolution say, "I'm going to love that so-and-so if it kills me." It just doesn't work that way. This harvest is cultivated as is any other harvest. First the ground has to be made ready. The readiness required is an open mind. There are many different ways God has of opening minds to His Word. A very common one is the realization of the horrendous responsibility of raising children. Many people come to the Church hoping to find help in this task. Others come in misfortune, or, much less frequently, out of thanksgiving. But the mind opens and the process begins. Then the seed must be planted. This corresponds to exposure to the concepts of the faith, through hearing, through reading, and through discussion, and like the cultivation in horticulture, has to be regularly done. And the harvest comes gradually, over the course of a lifetime. Slowly, almost imperceptibly, changes are made, and a person becomes new. It is grace that brings this about.

There is a concept about the Church which is characteristically Catholic called the doctrine of indefectibility. The Church is made of hopefully repentant sinners and some repent more completely than others. So sometimes perfectly terrible things are done by or in the name of the Church. But we do believe the Church is indefectible, which means, roughly, that no matter how evil the people are within it, no matter how bad the preaching, no matter what, a person who wants to receive the gospel will receive it. Therefore, if your church is all of these bad things and more, stay with it. Get up and go on some of those mornings you would rather stay in bed. Chances are that the priest would too. Go and spend the hour with God, even if Sunday is the only day you have to yourself—to play golf, to go fishing. If you are determined to receive the gospel you will.

We have never, as a Church, truly trusted in the teachings of Jesus and of St. Paul in the matters of grace versus the law. We have only partly learned our lesson. We slip back into being legalistic, moralistic and judgmental. And when we do so we not only lose the freedom so dearly bought us on the cross, but we betray our Lord by making the Church unattractive and forbidding when it should be joyous and inviting. It rejects when it needs to accept. But, as St. Paul says:

Law intruded into this process to multiply lawbreaking. But where sin was thus multiplied, grace immeasurably exceeded it. . . .

(Rom. 5:20 NEB)

Discussion Guide

In the introduction to this chapter, I spoke glowingly of freedom from anger, freedom from guilt and freedom from anxiety. I don't mean to imply that there are not times when fresh angers, guilts, and anxieties won't beset us again. But the means to freedom is always there. Ponder this manifesto on freedom from St. Paul.

The conclusion of the matter is this: there is no condemnation for those who are united with Christ Jesus, because in Christ Jesus the life-giving law of the Spirit has set you free from the law of sin and death. What the law could never do, because our lower nature robbed it of all potency, God has done: by sending his own Son in a form like that of our own sinful nature, and as a sacrifice for sin, he has passed judgement against sin within that very nature, so that the commandment of the law may find fulfilment in us, whose conduct, no longer under the control of our lower nature, is directed by the Spirit.

Those who live on the level of our lower nature have their outlook formed by it, and that spells death; but those who live on the level of the spirit have the spiritual outlook, and that is life and peace. For the outlook of the lower nature is enmity with God; it is not subject to the law of God; indeed it cannot be: those who live on such a level cannot possibly please God.

But that is not how you live. You are on the spiritual level, if only God's Spirit dwells within you; and if a man does not possess the Spirit of Christ, he is no Christian. But if Christ is dwelling within you, then although the body is a dead thing because you sinned, yet the spirit is life itself because you have been justified. Moreover, if the Spirit of him who raised Jesus from the dead dwells within you, then the God who raised Christ Jesus from the dead will also give new life to your mortal bodies through his indwelling Spirit.

(Rom. 8:1-11 NEB)

What does God tell you here about the means to freedom? How do you find it? Is it possible to lose it? How? *CLUE*: read just six verses before—Romans 7:19-20. The secret of the freedom is in this passage quoted. Has anyone perfectly achieved it in this life, aside from Jesus? Has Paul? If you think so, why does he say, "It is not to be thought that I have already achieved all this. I have not yet reached perfection, but I press on, hoping to take hold of that for which Christ once took hold of me" (Phil. 3:12)? How does that make you feel?

13

The Finger of God

The matter of this chapter is pictorially represented in Michelangelo's painting of the creation of Adam on the dome of the Sistine Chapel. It shows the finger of God touching the forefinger of the fully created Adam representing the completion of God's work of creating mankind. The purpose of the chapter is to show the almighty power of the finger of God, first as it is manifested in the Bible, then in the person of Jesus and finally manifested in men and women as devils have been cast out of them through the ages, in the hope that you will recognize the finger of God casting out demons in you. God has left with His Church the authority to bind or loose, which is exercised through the sacrament of penance. But God's grace, the liberating power we discussed in the last chapter, while it is operative through the sacraments, it is not limited to them. God is God and His grace is His grace and it is operative wherever He wills. It may well have been operative in anyone's life, casting out the demons which torment men and women without their awareness that it is the finger of God which furnishes the power. It is my hope that this chapter will help you discern the power of God operative in you so that you may consciously call upon it.

The phrase "finger of God" has been used occasionally

in the Old Testament to designate the creative power of the Almighty. The earliest user of the phrase is our old friend, D., who put it in the mouth of Moses as an explanation of the writing of the Ten Commandments: "The Lord gave me the two tablets of stone written with the finger of God" (Deut. 9:10 NEB).

P. put the phrase in the mouth of the magicians in Egypt who have been bested by Moses and Aaron: " 'It is the finger of God,' said the magicians to Pharaoh" (Exod. 8:19 NEB).

An unknown singer, joyful in the reestablishment of Jerusalem upon the return from the Babylonian captivity, used the phrase beautifully in a hymn of praise.

> When I consider thy heavens, even the work of thy fingers; the moon and stars which thou hast ordained;
>
> What is man, that thou art mindful of him? and the son of man, that thou visitest him?
>
> (Ps. 8:3-4d PBCP)

But it remained for Jesus to put the phrase into a different context.

> He was driving out a devil which was dumb; and when the devil had come out, the dumb man began to speak. The people were astonished, but some of them said, 'It is by Beelzebub prince of devils that he drives the devils out.' Others, by way of a test, demanded of him a sign from heaven. But he knew what was in their minds, and said, 'Every kingdom divided against itself goes to ruin, and a divided household falls. Equally, if Satan is divided himself, how can his kingdom stand?—since, as you would have it, I drive out the devils by Beelzebub. If it is by Beelzebub that I cast out devils, by whom do your own people drive them out? If this is your argument, they themselves would refute you. But

if it is by the finger of God that I drive out the devils, then be sure the kingdom of God has already come upon you.

(Luke 11:14-20 NEB)

I have written the whole episode because I wanted to put Jesus' use of the phrase in question into its context. First-century Palestine was an area in which superstition abounded, with a very general feeling that there was a devil behind every bush, and whenever a man suffered a disorder, physical or mental, it was attributed to demonic possession. The practice of exorcism (casting out devils) was common and there were many practitioners (exorcists) in the Jewish community. It was quite natural for some of those present to attribute the power over demons to Beelzebub and to accuse Jesus of trading on this power.

The term Beelzebub (the Lord of flies) is one of contempt, a play on the name Baalzebul (the lord of the temple) which the Canaanites gave to one of their deities. Jesus' logic is unanswerable, pointing out that Satan would never allow his power to be used for a good or healing purpose. He then supports his contention by referring to the Jewish exorcists who would deny any link with the prince of darkness in the exercise of their powers. This whole reference to "your own people" is suspect and many scholars feel it is not part of the earliest tradition. Certainly it is unlikely that Jesus would attribute the power of the finger of God to the Jewish exorcists who had no real power. He makes it clear, however, in his argument, that devils can only be cast out by the finger of God, and because he has that power, the kingdom of God has already come upon them. This is a claim similar to the one made in a previous chapter, namely, "This day is this scripture fulfilled in your ears" (Luke 4:21). Jesus is representing to His hearers that the power of God, associated with the kingdom of God, is present here and now in His coming. Moreover, this was power that He delegated to His apostles.

> On one of his teaching journeys round the villages he summoned the Twelve and sent them out in pairs on a mission. He gave them authority over unclean spirits. . . .
>
> (Mark 6:7 NEB)

This power of the finger of God in Jesus is human power, given to Jesus through His voluntary conformity to God's will. It is power that has been passed on from generation to generation through the Church.

One manifestation of the use of this power has been the Church's use of it to cast out the seven devils that can possess men and destroy them. While these are called the seven deadly sins, they are not really sins at all but attitudes of mind which are productive of sin. I take very seriously the power of the finger of God to cast out these devils. One of the very vivid sensations of my life was when the bishop and a dozen or so of my brother priests laid their hands on my head as these words were being said:

> Receive the Holy Ghost for the Office and Work of a Priest in the Church of God, now committed unto thee by the Imposition of our hands. Whose sins thou dost forgive, they are forgiven; and whose sins thou dost retain, they are retained. And be thou a faithful Dispenser of the Word of God, and of his holy Sacraments; in the Name of the Father, and of the Son, and of the Holy Ghost. Amen.
>
> (The Ordinal BCP, p. 546)

It seemed to me that I felt the weight of twenty centuries as the pressure of those many hands seemed about to push me through the floor. And ever since, the place where I feel most completely that the finger of God has taken me over and that the Holy Spirit possesses me is when I am dealing with these seven devils as they torment human souls. It is here the streaks of light are the most illuminating.

One of the insights that has come to me is that God has given men certain qualities or capacities which are neutral in themselves, neither good nor evil, but the value of them is determined by the way the individual soul uses them. Below are seven of these.

1. Regard for self
2. Regard for others
3. Reaction to evil
4. Appetite for food and drink
5. Appetite for sex
6. Appetite for things
7. Appetite for work

In the language of the English Reformation the spectrum of the regard for self ranged between humility as the virtue and pride as the sin. Our language today has almost exchanged the meanings of these two words. Pride means today a kind of self-respect which was certainly involved in a proper humility of the sixteenth century, but pride used to mean a swelling or an inflation. Humility, on the other hand has come in our time to be identified with servility or bootlicking, which is an ancient aspect of pride. So in dealing with this category I use reality and unreality in regard to self.

One of the very good legacies of our present-day way of thinking to the future is our current interpretation of the summary of the law.

> Thou shalt love the Lord thy God with all thy heart, and with all thy soul, and with all thy mind. This is the first and great commandment. And the

second is like unto it; Thou shalt love thy neighbour as thyself. On these two commandments hang all the Law and the Prophets.

(PBCP, p. 324)

The all too prevalent notion of several preceding generations has been that in order to be a good Christian, one must be a professional doormat. There was an unwillingness to take the commandment literally but rather to interpret it as to "love thy neighbor more than thyself" and to believe that one was being humble in doing so. This is fully as wrong as "to love thy neighbor less than thyself." The commandment says "as thyself" and that is what it means. So when you have a large need and your neighbor has a small, conflicting one, you meet yours. But if your need is small and your neighbor's large, you meet his.

It is the magnitude of the need that determines the priority, not to whom it belongs. But the person who does not love himself and does not have a realistic self-esteem, is unable to give love to anyone else. He feels that he is worthless; therefore, the love he gives is worthless. There are few things as corrosive and destructive to the well-being of the human soul as low self-esteem. And to move into the area of our discussion, it represents a most unrealistic regard for self. To begin with, every human soul has upon it the imprint of the image of God, made by Him for His purposes. To deny this is to accuse God of being a lousy creator. It is worthy of note that generally retarded children have engaging personalities, and usually they are not troubled by low self-esteem. And in the love, loyalty and devotion they often manifest, the image of God can be clearly seen.

But low self-esteem is not the only devil that exists from an unrealistic regard for self. Indeed this unreality is at the root of all sin, for in order to sin the sinner must say, in one form or another, "I know you don't want me to do this, God, but I am going to do it anyway." What could be more unrealistic in terms of self-regard than for the creature to presume to set himself over the creator in matters of right and wrong. Obviously, then, the devil of unreality in regard for self is cast out by becoming more intensely realistic. It is quite important to be realistic about one's good qualities as well as one's faults. I have asked regular penitents to confess their good qualities and good actions as well as their sins, in order to thank God for them, and to build on them. And spiritual health consists in moving behavior in regard for self from the unrealistic to the realistic side of things.

How do we regard the good fortune of others? Do we rejoice with them or are we envious of them, even though we might not want what they have achieved. Or, conversely, I remember well as a child my rejoicing when my sister got spanked. And here we have the poles of the spectrum of regard for others—joy on the one hand and envy on the other. Envy is a terrible poison, which not only destroys the capacity for sharing in the joy of others, but destroys all joy whatsoever, because the person is so preoccupied with being envious about others that he has not time or energy for experiencing joy on his own. But the remedy is the same. The attitude of the soul must change so that he can begin to experience joy in his life.

Quite often envy is tied to low self-esteem, as these devils love company and often come in a group. It is said, (mythologically) that the only two of the deadly sins that Satan can commit are pride and envy, and these he did commit at the moment of his creation, when he was dazzled by his own beauty and envious of the role of God the Son as the Savior of the world. But for whatever reason, these two devils seem often to work as a team.

A capacity which seems to differ from all the others is the capacity to react to evil. The emotional steam which is always part of this reaction is what we call anger and has been misleadingly and mistakenly called one of the deadly sins. The problem with anger is not that we have the reaction, but that we use it in a destructive way, in trying to punish or annihilate the evildoer, rather than to eliminate the evil being done. Unfortunately, the impression has been given that a Christian does not get angry, in spite of Jesus' quite healthy display of anger in dealing with the money changers and other religious racketeers in the Temple. As a result, angers that need expression are suppressed by many with resulting psychic damage. The whole of the capacity can be properly called anger, with efficient, constructive use of it at one extreme, and vindictive, destructive use of it at the other. And the devil generated by the latter, particularly when it is unrecognized within the person, is a terror indeed. And before he can be cast out—the source of the anger, that is—the evil causing it must be identified. Then the energy of anger must be channeled to bring about the elimination of the evil, and in so far as possible, its effects. However, this is not always possible, because often the effects of evil are irreversible. Therefore, the ultimate way to deal with anger and the only way effectively to remove its sting is in forgiveness.

The remaining four capacities have to do with various kinds of appetites. The problem with appetites in general is that they tend to become obsessive. This is especially true of the appetite for food and drink. The old admonition, "Eat to live, don't live to eat" is a very meaningful one, because as a formerly fat man, I know from experience the kind of preoccupation with food that goes with obesity. Also, persons build dependencies on food and, more particularly, on alcohol. So the span is between self-control and gluttony, and self-knowledge is one of the important ingredients in bringing about self-control. If a person begins to understand the origins of his compulsions he is well on the road to bringing them to heel.

The appetite for sex is somewhat different. Its proper indulgence is in the expression of a meaningful, secure, relationship between a couple committed to each other in love. While it does not guarantee that these things will always be present, the institution of marriage is the frame in which they are generally expected. In such a situation, the virtuous pole of the spectrum is purity, in terms of a full strength, unadulterated relationship. The other pole is lust, which is the exploitive, self-indulgent, and casual use of the sex act. Unfortunately, the Church has not done a good job of teaching our young any solid, basic reasons for confining sex to marriage.

The sin is not in indulging sexual appetites outside the framework of marriage, but in qualities of exploitation, casualness or irresponsibility that are much more likely to be a feature of extramarital sex than of sex within wedlock. Moreover, the appetite for sex can lend itself very well to an obsessive-compulsive kind of expression, and as in the matter of food and drink, self-awareness is the beginning of dealing with problems of lust.

The appetite for things gives rise to various kinds of idolatries. There is a rather common saying which advises us to "use things to love people rather than to use people to get things." This cuts right to the heart of the matter, because if a person covets that which belongs to his neighbor long enough and hard enough, he will somehow exploit persons to get it. Actually the range here is between generosity and covetousness. The idolatry comes in when the value we set on things causes us to do that which we know is displeasing to God to acquire them. Obviously, this is the worship of a thing, whatever it may be, at the expense of the worship of God. Worship is essentially "worth ship" or assigning value to the object of veneration. It is not always, or necessarily, done in a formal situation kneeling meekly on your knees.

The appetite for work is a strange one. The devil of inefficiency, or procrastination, whatever you want to call it, was called sloth originally but has unfortunately come to be synonymous with laziness. But the person caught in this trap is not lazy. I have the greatest success in explaining this to women by talking about the ironing pile. It works like this. The ironing pile is huge, so large that when the housewife sees it she is exhausted and goes to take a nap. When she wakes up it is too late to tackle the ironing, but she has an attack of guilt which makes her more tired than before she took the nap. And things get worse and worse, as she becomes more and more guilty, until she finally pulls herself together and gets everything done. But then she really is exhausted and the process begins all over again. The trick is to cultivate a high level of efficiency which evens out the work so that by daily diligence it can be accomplished.

As I have written this it all seems rather prosaic to me, and presumptuous, compared with our Lord's casting out the demons and restoring speech to the dumb. Yet these are demons, capable singly or in groups of destroying us. Moreover, I have seen the finger of God cast them out.

Discussion Guide

Has this chapter helped you to discern the finger of God operative in your life? Perhaps you can think of an instance you would like to talk about. I like to think of the finger of God nudging me toward humility, joy, forgiveness, temperance, purity, generosity, and diligence. But we all know there are devils to cast out first. Is the mere casting out of devils enough? Jesus says something on the subject.

'When an unclean spirit comes out of a man it wanders over the deserts seeking a resting-place; and if it finds none, it says, "I will go back to the home I left." So it returns and finds the house swept clean, and tidy. Off it goes and collects seven other spirits more wicked than itself, and they all come in and settle down; and in the end the man's plight is worse than before.'

(Luke 11:24-26 NEB)

What is Jesus telling us here? Have you experienced what He means? How can we find resources to fill our houses now that they are swept and tidy? What streaks of light does God offer for this purpose? Is the Bible the only source? How do we find help in our worship? Our life of prayer? Within the fellowship of Christians?

14

Three Long Hours

The purpose of this chapter is to bring us face to face with Jesus as the Bible straightforwardly and with great restraint describes His passion and death. We are caught up in this and cannot escape cringing and cowering as we feel the brutality and depravity of the world's evil as it brings itself to bear on the perfect goodness of Jesus. Our own ills are nothing to us, and our reactions shameful as the beaten and battered figure retains all the dignity God meant for man to possess.

We cannot face this scene unmoved. We cannot be involved in it without being aware that we, too, have added our sins to the burden of the cross. But the reality is that the guilt has been taken away. We may not choose to let go of it, but we were saved from it on that cross. "With his stripes we are healed" (Isa. 53:5 KJV).

Coming face to face with Jesus on the cross makes us new men and women in Him. This is what I hope this chapter will strengthen and support.

The three long hours Jesus spent dying on the cross represented a climax, a distillate, a summary in a sense of His entire earthly life. The Crucifixion ought not to be looked at as a separate event in His life but rather as an inevitable consequence of the way He lived. The model of listening and obeying on which Jesus patterned His life was brought to its logical conclusion in the complete self-giving on the cross.

But in the twenty-four hours before the Crucifixion itself Jesus underwent enough mental torment and physical abuse to kill a man. One can't imagine the feelings of our Lord at the Last Supper, acting out the offering of himself He was to make the next day. What doubts crossed His mind as He looked upon the twelve, those He had chosen to carry on His work, and He saw their weaknesses and inadequacies? What was it like to know that the leader He would leave in His place was a hopeless coward—or to eat His last meal with His betrayer? We must believe that Jesus was more, rather than less, sensitive to these things than we would be. His will to live resisted with all its power against His inevitable destiny. The agony in the garden of Gethsemane indicated that.

> Father, if it be thy will, take this cup away from me. Yet not my will but thine be done.
>
> (Luke 22:42 NEB)

When one reads the account of the seizure and trial of Jesus in the New English Bible one is struck by the vicious brutality of the whole business. The archaic language of the King James Version takes the edge off this. Jesus was physically beaten at least three times the night before He died, once by His guards, once by Herod's men, and finally Pilate had Him flogged before sending Him out to be crucified. We can be sure that the sting of these beatings was characteristic of the malevolence of evil in the face of goodness, that the beatings themselves were vicious beyond those administered to an ordinary criminal. They had the steam of ridicule and contempt behind them.

The holy shroud of Turin is mute testimony to all this. Tradition has it that this is the shroud in which Jesus was wrapped when He was so hastily entombed so that the holy days beginning at sundown Good Friday would not be desecrated. There was no time to prepare the body for burial so over fifty pounds of aloes and myrrh (John 19:39) were applied to the body to retard spoilage and then it was hastily enfolded in a linen shroud fourteen feet long and three feet wide. The tradition is that the shroud was carefully taken from the empty tomb and preserved. It journeyed from Jerusalem to Constantinople, was taken to France by the Crusaders, rescued from a fire and finally reached its present resting place in Turin, Italy.

Whatever its origin, the shroud has always had a number of very light brown stains and a number of darker ones of varying sizes. These stains, barely discernible to the eye, form an image of a man, front and back, very much like a photographic negative. As a matter of fact, it remained for the development of the science of photography to tell the full story of the shroud. The mysterious chemistry of aloes, myrrh, human perspiration, blood shed while the man was alive, blood from a wound in his side after he was dead, all furnished a plausible explanation of how the shroud could be stained with the image.

The Church has never proclaimed the genuineness of the shroud, nor has she denied it. Almost every Pope since Julius II (1503-1513) has believed in its authenticity. Its greatest support has come not from a continuous tradition but from the emergence of scientific tools of verification. There is more support for it now than ever before, and I am going to use its testimony to support what I have written about the night before the Crucifixion.

The shroud shows a man of muscular build with a terribly battered face. His nose has obviously been recently broken. There is a large bruise over his left eye, another on his left cheekbone which has almost caused his eye to be swollen shut. There is also a prominent bump on his jaw. Obviously these were vicious blows which John describes, "Then time after time, they came up to him crying, 'Hail, King of the Jews!', and struck him on the face" (John 19:3 NEB).

The crown of thorns was more a cap than a crown, as the blood stains attest, not only on the crown of his head, but also on top. It would seem that the cap was jammed on his head, causing wounds all over. Scourgings were administered by a flagellum which was made by attaching two leather thongs about three feet long to a stout wooden handle. At the end of each thong was an object which looked like a miniature barbell an inch and a quarter long made of metal or bone. Every time a blow was struck, the barbell left two cuts, one from each end of the device, leaving four for each time the whip fell. These appear on the shroud as small stains of blood, beginning at the shoulders and chest and working systematically down to the calves of his legs. One can account for sixty-three blows of the whip on the shroud. Such is the testimony of what some people call the Fifth Gospel, the holy shroud of Turin.

Dom Gregory Dix speculates on the situation in which Jesus uttered the first of His seven last words. Was it at the moment when His hands were being nailed to the patibulum, or crosspiece? The agony of this moment was so excruciating that at crucifixions it customarily took four men to accomplish the task. We can imagine Jesus, unresisting, saying these words: "Father, forgive them; they do not know what they are doing" (Luke 23:34 NEB).

Or was it, as Dom Gregory suggests, at that instant when the crosspiece was lifted high in the air and then fixed in its place with a jarring thud, so that the weight of the body, supported for the first time by the wounds themselves tore them anew. Then the feet were put one on top of the other and nailed to a small footrest on the upright. Perhaps this is a little unnecessarily graphic and bloody, but the reality of the cross is difficult for us. This was the execution of a criminal. I have a priest friend who has an ambition to preach Good Friday with an electric chair on the altar. This would certainly bring the reality of the cross into our day. But for Jesus to be able to pray in such a moment for His executioners moves the injunctions of the Sermon on the Mount from theoretical speech into agonizing action.

As the suffering grew, the crowd added to Jesus' misery with its taunts. While He realized that His bitter cup must be drained to the bottom, this knowledge did not lessen the sting in the words of the ignorant: "He saved others: now let him save himself, if this is God's Messiah, his Chosen" (Luke 23:35 NEB).

Even one of the thieves joins the taunting mob: "Are not you the Messiah? Save yourself, and us" (Luke 23:39 NEB).

Somehow this aroused in the other thief a sense of sympathy and provoked him to say: "Have you no fear of God. You are under the same sentence as he. For us it is plain justice: we are paying the price for our misdeeds; but this man has done nothing wrong."

He then addressed himself to Jesus: "Jesus remember me when you come to your throne" (Luke 23:41-42 NEB).

I recall once listening to a sermon on this word of the cross which began like this:

"And then Jesus looked over at the thief with great understanding and compassion. He carefully appraised his character and satisfying himself he said: 'I tell you this: today you shall be with me in Paradise.' He knew that he was a straight shooter!"

Of all the many legitimate comments which might be made on this verse, the above certainly is not one of them. Our Lord made this promise to the penitent thief precisely because he was not a straight shooter. He was a thief who knew he deserved what he got, and said so. Obviously he was sorry. But for my colleague preacher, no one was about to get into Paradise who hadn't earned it. I have often wondered how he might preach on this phrase of St. Paul's:

> Here are words you may trust, words that merit full acceptance: 'Christ Jesus came into the world to save sinners'; and among them I stand first.
>
> (1 Tim. 1:15 NEB).

Another of Dom Gregory's pithy observations centers around the next word of the cross. He describes the thinning of the crowd to the point that Mary the mother of Jesus, Mary Magdalene and the apostle John are left at the foot of the cross. Then he notes that this is the way things go in the Church. The last to leave are the completely virtuous, the utterly repentant and the clergy.

In his words to his mother:

> Mother, there is your son.

And to St. John:

> There is your mother.
>
> (John 19:27 NEB)

He makes provision for both. Widows, in Jesus' day, without children to support them, begged or starved, so in giving His mother a son, He was assuring her future. John, too, was young and still in need of a mother.

The next word of the cross is the most startling. Yet, its full impact is not always felt. I believe that people hear it with bewilderment and dismiss it without trying to perceive its meaning. Recently I was preaching on this word, as the fifth address in a three-hour service.

The congregation was getting a little tired of preaching by then. I deliberately droned on painting a word picture of the darkening day, with its few hangers on, the soldiers, bored with crucifixions in general, engaged in a crap game at the foot of the cross. And then at the top of my lungs I announced my text: "My God! My GOD!! WHY hast thou forsaken me?" Then the congregation, as one person, seemed to rise a foot off the pew.

This word is testimony to the complete humanity of Jesus. He had no way of knowing the outcome of the Crucifixion other than by His faith. And here, in the moment of His deepest agony, when the issue was least certain, He did what human beings do. He doubted. It is not a sin to doubt. Often the doubt serves as a call from God to a greater faith.

It is worth making a connection between the statement "Thou shalt love thy neighbor as thyself" and the priorities of needs suggested in the last chapter, and Jesus' living of this commandment on the cross. The basic need He wanted to fulfill was the need of all men for salvation, and it was this He was making the effort to meet. But, in addition, He was concerned for the need of His tormentors for forgiveness and He prayed for it. He saw the need of the penitent thief for absolution and He gave it. He met the mutual need of His mother and beloved disciple, for support and companionship. It was only then that He concerned himself with a need of His own, a spiritual one. And finally, after dealing with His doubt, He faced His physical need.

I thirst.

(John 19:29 NEB)

It was at the very end, at the bottom of Jesus' system of priorities, that He faced the demands of His body. And yet they were real, as intense as physical need can be.

It was then that He gave the triumphant cry: *Tetelestai!*
> (John 19:30 Wescott and Hort)

I had promised myself I was not going to put any Greek in this book. But it is one word in Greek which requires almost a paragraph in English to transmit its meaning. The basic verb is the one that you would use to describe a fruit getting ripe, or a plan brought to maturity. One might translate this word, "The plan begun so long ago has been brought to a conclusion and finally accomplished its purpose." The King James Version says, "It is finished"; the New English Bible, "It is accomplished." The German Bible translates it, "*Es ist vollbracht.*" All approach the meaning but lack the note of triumph of the original. The best of all is the paraphrase of Father Bonnell Spencer of the Order of the Holy Cross: "I've done it!"

The final word, spoken in a phrase from the Psalms, (Ps. 31:5) summarizes the complete self-surrender acted out on the cross.

Father, into thy hands I commit my spirit.
> (Luke 23:46 NEB)

What does it all mean? I have been very sketchy, even random, in my comments about these three long hours that changed the course of the world. But it is not the minutiae that is important. It is the overarching meaning. What does the death of a young religious revolutionary by execution twenty centuries ago have to do with me or you?

The classic view is that man through his own perverseness and through the power of the devil and his cohorts over him has become enslaved and cannot free himself. Christ comes into the world, strives with these powers throughout his life, in the temptations he has in common with other men, and finally on the cross, enduring all that the devil can put upon him, and still triumphs over him. This victory over the worst that Satan can do brings to men redemption from the dark powers that have held them captive. This sounds very mythological, but examine the realities behind this view. John Macquarrie, in his fine book, *Principles of Christian Theology*, points out that the root sin of man, that by which he primarily distorts his nature, is idolatry. This does not mean that he makes unto himself graven images and bows down and worships them, but that, in Paul Tillich's meaningful phrase, he makes an ultimate concern of something that is not ultimate.

The early Christian church believed that when a person involved himself in idolatry, the idol itself took on demonic powers which ultimately destroyed or enslaved the worshiper. There is a way in which this is quite profoundly true. Certainly the idolatry of Macbeth in worshiping his growing ambition, created a force in his life that can only be described as diabolical and which led to his ultimate destruction. What is true of individuals can be equally true of a people. History abounds with examples of nations who made a god of their military power, and as a consequence of this idolatry their people have deteriorated morally to an amazing degree. The consequences seem to reach into all areas of human existence with corroding, bestializing force.

The ultimate idolatry of the human being is the worship of himself. In His death on the cross, Jesus successfully resisted the temptation to do His own will rather than the Father's thus avoiding this idolatry of self-worship and thereby achieving the ultimate in obedience and self-offering. The whole of the power of evil was brought to bear on His person and He steadfastly refused to submit to it. While this action took place once and for all at a specific place and time in human history, the effect of this victory takes place in a continuing way in the lives of men and women today. The opportunity comes to every man many times in his life to take up his cross and follow Jesus. Each one of us faces a personal crucifixion during which the power of Christ's triumph is made available to us through our faith in its saving qualities. The victorious lives of many saints known and unknown are testimony to this power. However, even though this saving energy is available to us it is not forced upon us. We must cooperate with it within ourselves by action of our own wills.

Men are inspired by the cross to follow Jesus' example and live a life in imitation of Him. However, this inspiration would not be enough in itself to account for the unimaginable effect the power of the cross has had on so many human lives in the twenty centuries since the Crucifixion. There has to be another dimension active within this saving force, one which transcends man's capacity to follow an example or live by imitation. This dimension must be supplied by God himself.

Man's very earliest religious experiences were always involved with sacrifice, with returning to God a token of what God had given to him, not so much in order to make it holy as to acknowledge its holiness. There were two motives behind this. The one was gratitude for what was bestowed upon man by processes he could not understand. He knew that food to sustain him in life was available to him in nature, but he did not contribute himself to its availability.

The sacrifice had the function of acknowledgment and thanksgiving for the gift. Yet there would be times of famine when game was scarce or the land was dry. Man would, in such times, feel alienated from the force that fed him and seek through his sacrifice to be reconciled. So whether through gratitude or guilt, or both, sacrifices have been made and are woven into the fabric of religion as it exists today. The sacrifice, very early, was offered by the priest on behalf of the sacrificer, which brought about a reconciliation with God that the believer could not effect on his own.

Christ on the cross functioned as both priest and victim, thereby freeing men from the force of evil against which they are powerless on their own. Moreover, the self-giving of Christ as God incarnate acting in human history represents the complete self-giving of God which is the essence of His nature and the source of His creating and sustaining activities. So it is power of God on the cross effecting the reconciliation between himself and man, needing only the cooperation of each individual human will to bring it about.

In the course of the history of the Christian era there have been many and diverse varieties of the followers of Christ, who have disagreed, sometimes violently, on the meanings of the Christian religion. But there is one faith they hold in common which unites them as Christians. Jesus Christ's death on the cross saves men. It saves you.

In the face of this great fact, theological speculations are flat and meaningless. In the biblical account of the passion we live close to the person of Christ. We suffer with Him because He suffers for us. When one reads the passion narratives according to all four evangelists during holy week, one cannot help being changed. One of the magnificent choruses from the Messiah comes flooding into the mind.
'Worthy is the Lamb, the Lamb that was slain, to receive all power and wealth, wisdom and might, honour and glory and praise.'
(Rev. 5:12 NEB)

The reassuring voice of Juliana of Norwich echoes in the depth of consciousness, "All will be well, will be well and will be well." Like looking through the big end of a telescope, we see a tiny vision of Teilhard de Chardin's *Omega Point*, when the whole world will be the body of Christ, coming into focus. The fact that I am saved blends into the whole picture. The world has been saved for all who will it. One wants to say with St. Augustine, *O felix culpa!* "O happy sin that bought so great a salvation."

I can't bring myself to call this a Discussion Guide. The passion of our Lord Jesus Christ is not something that can be profitably discussed, pro and con. Shared, yes, but not discussed. The most meaningful way to consider the passion is to meditate on it a bit at a time. Let us begin here.

When he reached the place he said to them, 'Pray that you may be spared the hour of testing.' He himself withdrew from them about a stone's throw, knelt down, and began to pray: 'Father, if it be thy will, take this cup away from me. Yet not my will but thine be done.'

And now there appeared to him an angel from heaven bringing him strength, and in anguish of spirit he prayed the more urgently; and his sweat was like clots of blood falling to the ground.

When he rose from prayer and came to the disciples he found them asleep, worn out by grief. 'Why are you sleeping?' he said. 'Rise and pray that you may be spared the test.'

(Luke 22:40-46 NEB)

Even at the time of His greatest trial, Jesus has something to say for us. What do you make of His words to the disciples before He went off to pray? Do you see a meaning beyond what they may face in the next twenty-four hours? What does this say to you? How does it apply to all men?

What do we learn from Jesus' prayer? What is the significance of God's angel coming to strengthen Him? What does this tell us of the efficacy of prayer? Bloody sweat is a medically recognized phenomenon, sometimes characteristic of soldiers going into battle. Again He finds the disciples asleep.

Think of the times Jesus has wanted your attention and vigilance. How have you failed Him? How can we resolve this conflict in us between the willingness of the spirit and the weakness of the flesh?

15

Emmaus and Afterwards

The resurrection experience is the key to our faith. While the Bible has many accounts of our Lord's appearances after the Resurrection, each with its own invitation to faith, our real conviction comes from our own encounter with the risen Lord. This chapter recounts some of these biblical appearances to you in a way which I hope will help make the risen Christ accessible to you. This is the gift of the witnesses of the Resurrection to us. The vividness and power of their testimony opens us to their experience. The history of the Church abounds with witnesses to the risen Lord at all times and in all places. This is not confined to saints but is the legacy of those whom Dom Gregory Dix has called *plebs sancta Dei*, the holy common people of God. This book is written because of the conviction that the risen Lord does make himself manifest to men in those streaks of light available to us all. Many experience the risen Lord without realizing it. Perhaps this chapter will help you recognize Him for who He is, as one you already know.

The Crucifixion was a public event. The episode in the life of Jesus most strongly supported by solid historical evidence is His execution under Pontius Pilate. The passion narratives in all four Gospels are completely detailed. In contrast to this we are told repeatedly that, "God raised him to life again, setting him free from the pangs of death" (Acts 2:24 NEB). (See also Acts 4:10; 10:40; Rom. 4:24, and many other places.) As we have said, many people saw the Crucifixion as an act in history; many testified to their encounter with the resurrected Lord; but only God, who raised Him from the dead, was present at that event. It is not accessible to us through human witness.

The accounts of the post-Resurrection appearances of Jesus are as hazy and confused as those of the passion are graphic and detailed. This is said not to cast doubt on the Resurrection, but to point out that it was a unique phenomenon, seen differently by many beholders to whom it had extraordinary significance. Moreover, in the retelling, the records gathered details supplied to meet the needs of the infant Christian community in refuting its adversaries. An example of such is found in St. Matthew:

> The women had started on their way when some of the guard went into the city and reported to the chief priests everything that had happened. After meeting with the elders and conferring together, the chief priests offered the soldiers a substantial bribe and told them to say, 'His disciples came by night and stole the body while we were asleep.' They added, 'If this should reach the Governor's ears, we will put matters right with him and see that you do not suffer.' So they took the money and did as they were told. This story became widely known, and is current in Jewish circles to this day.
> (Matt. 28:11-15 NEB)

Another factor contributing to the confusion surrounding the post-Resurrection appearances of Jesus grows out of differing views of Jew and Greek toward life after death. The Hebrew believed that body and soul were inextricably bound together, so that when the body died, the soul died with it. Therefore, when they anticipated life after death, they thought in terms of a bodily resurrection, because they could not conceive of a soul without a body to be the vehicle of its expression. Moreover, the Jews looked upon the human body as one of the wonders of God's creation and believed thoroughly in its goodness.

The Greeks, however, saw the body as the prison house of the soul, an evil thing which hampered the pure expression of the human spirit by its appetites and demands. So when the Greek contemplated the afterlife, he thought in terms of the immortality of the soul, freed at last from the tyranny of the body. It is quite easy to see that a person transmitting an account of a post-Resurrection appearance of Jesus would be understanding what he was telling in a way determined by whether he was Jew or Greek. Therefore, the accounts which seem to point to physical resurrection, those that mention touching the wounds and Jesus' eating are Jewish in origin, while those which talk in terms of going through locked doors and disappearing from sight seem to point to having been transmitted by Greeks.

Oddly enough, the earliest account of the post-Resurrection appearances, a scant twenty-five years after they took place, is not in the Gospels where we would expect it to be, but in Paul's first letter to the Corinthians. Paul summarized what must have been a well-established tradition in the words below:

> First and foremost, I handed on to you the facts which had been imparted to me: that Christ died for our sins, in accordance with the scriptures; that he was buried; that he was raised to life on the third day, according to the scriptures; and that he

appeared to Cephas, and afterwards to the Twelve. Then he appeared to over five hundred of our brothers at once, most of whom are still alive, though some have died. Then he appeared to James, and afterwards to all the apostles. In the end he appeared even to me.

(1 Cor. 15:3-8 NEB)

We should first remember that this is a summary of all the appearances traditionally known, and not a detailed account of any of them. So we can find indications in this summary of much that is told in more detail in the Gospels. It is significant that Paul specifically mentions the burial of Jesus, for it was not at all certain that an executed criminal would have been given proper burial. It also indicated that his tradition contained knowledge of Joseph of Arimathaea and his gift of the tomb, which is told in detail in each of the four Gospels. However, the statement, "That he was raised to life on the third day," does not substantiate the account of the empty tomb of which so much is made in the Gospels, for Paul is simply referring to the time God raised him up, appealing to the authority of Scripture, rather than alluding to the time of discovery of the Resurrection. Here is the Old Testament allusion which Paul believed alluded to Jesus' Resurrection.

Come, let us return to the Lord:
for he has torn us and will heal us,
he has struck us and he will bind up our wounds;
after two days he will revive us,
on the third day he will restore us,
that in his presence we may live.

(Hos. 6:1-2 NEB)

In Paul's account, it is to Peter (Cephas in Aramaic)

that Jesus first appeared. This seems to contradict the record in all the Gospels, (except Luke), of the experience of Mary Magdalene at the tomb, but there seems to be an echo of this appearance to Peter in Luke's Gospel:

> There they found that the Eleven and the rest of the company had assembled, and were saying, 'It is true: the Lord has risen; he has appeared to Simon.' (Luke 24:34 NEB)

Paul might also be referring to the account of the appearance to Peter and the other disciples in Galilee, found in John's Gospel in the twenty-first chapter. Since there is some evidence to support Paul's contention of an early appearance of the Lord to Peter and since Paul is silent about the appearance of the risen Christ to Mary Magdalene, it is possible he did not know of it.

It is impossible to tie definitely the other accounts of Paul with those in the Gospels, simply because he hasn't given us enough detail. However, we can conjecture that the mention of Jesus' appearing to over 500 must have taken place in Galilee because that was the only place that He might have been able to assemble that many of His followers. The appearance to James is not recorded elsewhere in the New Testament, although it does appear in the apocryphal gospel to the Hebrews. However, the prominence of James in the early Church certainly suggests that such an appearance took place. Indeed, the statement that "then . . . afterwards appeared to all the apostles" in the same verse does not necessarily mean that He appeared to them all at one time or that this appearance was limited to the twelve. Preceded by the appearance to James and followed by the telling of his own experience, it could well be that Paul meant this to indicate Jesus' specific way of calling these apostles to their ministry in the Church.

It would seem that Paul had no concept of the Ascension of Christ, as specifically told in Luke. The mythological character of the Ascension accounts in Luke and also the concept of a three-story universe they presuppose, indicate that these passages grew out of the need of the early Church to explain why Jesus did not continue to appear to latter day Christians, rather than from the record of an historic event.

Paul's summary of the post-Resurrection activities of Jesus is not only valuable because of the closeness to the events in time but also because it is an admirable combination of the Jewish and Greek views of life after death. Paul is a thoroughgoing Jew writing to a Greek audience. He is steadfast in his insistence on the appearance of Jesus himself in bodily form rather than appearing as some manner of vision or hallucination on the part of those who said they saw Him. The use of the verb "was seen," in the King James Bible, is an inaccurate translation of the Greek, and the New English Bible's insistence on an appearance ("he appeared") in an objective sense is correct. But, Paul is careful to phrase his summary in a way that will not offend the sensibilities of his Greek audience who would be repelled by the notion of a dead body being revived.*

While I accept and am moved in various ways by the accounts of Jesus' appearances to the apostles before the Ascension, I can identify most closely with Paul's statement, "In the end he appeared even to me. It was like an abnormal birth" (1 Cor. 15:8 NEB). Knowing

---

*I acknowledge my debt for many of the insights into these verses from 1 Cor. 15 discussed above to Clarence Tucker Craig in his fine exegesis on them in the *Interpreters' Bible*, Abingdon-Cokesbury Press, Nashville, 1954.

that the Lord does, even today, to us who are born out of due time, as Paul testifies, validate His appearance to me. I was not blinded by a vision or struck blind but the wordless voice spoke with shattering impact and I heard, and in the intervening years, have obeyed, sometimes more sometimes less. I was commissioned and the only way of escape is through disobedience. I know in my heart that the Lord is risen indeed; and because He appeared to me, I am convinced that He appeared to Paul, to Peter and to all the rest.

There is no parallel reference that can be identified with certainty in Paul that corresponds to the episode of the happening on the road to Emmaus told in detail by Luke and also alluded to in Mark (Mark 16:12-13). It could come from a tradition unknown to Paul, but I prefer to think that this appearance is one he refers to in a blanket way as to ". . . then afterwards appeared to all the apostles." Whatever the origin, it is one of the most interesting of the witnesses to the post-Resurrection appearances of Jesus.

That same day two of them were on their way to a village called Emmaus, which lay about seven miles from Jerusalem, and they were talking together about all these happenings. As they talked and discussed it with one another, Jesus himself came up and walked along with them; but something kept them from seeing who it was. He asked them, 'What is it you are debating as you walk?' They halted, their faces full of gloom, and one, called Cleopas, answered, 'Are you the only person staying in Jerusalem not to know what has happened there in the last few days?' 'What do you mean?' he said. 'All this about Jesus of Nazareth,' they replied, 'a prophet powerful in speech and action before God and the whole people; how our chief priests and rulers handed him over to be sentenced to death, and crucified him. But we had been hoping that he was the man to liberate Israel. What is more, this is the third day since it happened, and now some women of our company have astounded us: they went early to the tomb but failed to find his body, and returned with a story that they had seen a vision of angels who told them he was alive. So some of our people went to the tomb and found things just as the women had said; but him they did not see.'

'How dull you are!' he answered. 'How slow to believe all that the prophets said! Was the Messiah not bound to suffer thus before entering upon his glory?' Then he began with Moses and all the prophets, and explained to them the passages which referred to himself in every part of the scriptures.

By this time they had reached the village to which they were going, and he made as if to continue his journey, but they pressed him: 'Stay with us, for evening draws on, and the day is almost over. So he went in to stay with them. And when he had sat down with them at table, he took bread and said the blessing; he broke the bread, and offered it to them. Then their eyes were opened and they recognized him; and he vanished from their sight. They said to one another, 'Did we not feel our hearts on fire as he talked with us on the road and explained the scriptures to us?'

Without a moment's delay they set out and returned to Jerusalem. There they found that the Eleven and the rest of the company had assembled, and were saying, 'It is true: the Lord has risen; he has appeared to Simon.' Then they gave their account of the events of their journey and told how he had been recognized by them at the breaking of the bread. (Luke 24:13-35, NEB)

There is much that makes us wonder in this account. How, for example, was it that they did not recognize Jesus? Certainly St. Luke seems to imply that it was through some use of supernatural power that they were prevented from knowing who He was. But why was it necessary for them not at first to know Him? We can only conjecture here, but I imagine that if they had known Him, they would have been so overwhelmed by the wonder of His appearance that they would have been unable to learn what He was trying to teach them. I personally believe that this was one of the occasions Paul refers to when he says: "Then he appeared to James, and afterwards to all the apostles" (1 Cor. 15:7 NEB).

There is nothing in the way this passage is worded that requires us to believe that this was a single appearance at one place, and I want to emphasize, as I mentioned above, that Paul could see this as an individual commissioning of the apostles, (which included persons other than the twelve), much in the way that Jesus converted him. The Emmaus appearance would fit such a pattern. Since Jesus wished to prepare them for their ministry by expounding Scripture to them, He would not want them distracted by His appearance to them after rising from the dead.

Equally appropriate is the method He used to reveal himself to them, for in it He revealed to them another quality of the ongoing character of His Church, namely that in the taking of bread, blessing it, breaking it and offering it, as He commanded them in the Last Supper, by doing this they would recall Him among them at each successive Eucharist. We must believe, then, that this pattern, now the basis of every celebration of the Holy Communion, must have been characteristic of Jesus at every meal He shared with His friends, and not at the Last Supper alone, because these two He met on the road to Emmaus were not present at that time.

The mode in which our Lord is immediately asccessible to eucharistically centered Christians is in the breaking of the bread. Jesus' command to do this for His *Anamnesis*, ("Do this to recall the reality of my resurrected life in your life," might be a lengthy paraphrase) confronts us with the risen Lord, just as those at the supper in Emmaus were so confronted. Surely many of us receive our commission anew each time at the holy table, and are sent out "to do the work you have given us to do, to love and serve you as faithful witnesses of Christ, our Lord" (PBCP, p. 366).

In order to complete the identification of His appearance as the commissioning of new apostles to carry on the faith, we need to know who these two were and their place in the subsequent history of the Church. There is nothing in Scripture, or indeed very early in Church history to help us here, but there is mention in Eusebius, a historian of the late third and early fourth century, of an early tradition that it was Cleopas, (or Clopas, a later form of the name) and his son Simon, who afterwards succeeded James as bishop of Jerusalem.

It is as if St. Luke, having recalled an appearance which emphasized an unearthly, almost ghostly quality of the unrecognized Jesus on the road to Emmaus, immediately recounts another, which refutes, totally, any notion of a ghostly appearance.

> As they were talking about all this, there he was, standing among them. Startled and terrified, they thought they were seeing a ghost. But he said, 'Why are you so perturbed? Why do questionings

arise in your minds? Look at my hands and my feet. It is I myself. Touch me and see; no ghost has flesh and bones as you can see that I have.' They were still unconvinced, still wondering, for it seemed too good to be true. So he asked them, 'Have you anything here to eat?' They offered him a piece of fish they had cooked, which he took and ate before their eyes. (Luke 24:36-43 NEB)

So, in the space of thirty verses in the same Gospel we have two accounts of post-Resurrection appearances of Jesus which cover the whole range from the utterly earthly to other-worldly, spiritual concepts. Yet, behind each description there seems to be purpose, a desire to assure some aspect of the faith for transmission to future generations. But behind the descriptions is the tradition itself, with its insistence of the resurrection of the body in a persistent way that cannot be denied, and at the same time the equally tenacious tradition which asserts that the resurrected body is a glorified body, with qualities differing greatly from the human body as we know it. The balance between these two traditions is best stated by St. Paul:

But, you may ask, how are the dead raised? In what kind of body? How foolish! The seed you sow does not come to life unless it has first died; and what you sow is not the body that shall be, but a naked grain, perhaps of wheat, or of some other kind; and God clothes it with the body of his choice, each seed its own particular body. . . . So it is with the resurrection of the dead. What is sown in the earth as a perishable thing is raised imperishable. Sown in humiliation, it is raised in glory; sown in weakness, it is raised in power, sown as an animal body, it is raised as a spiritual body.
(1 Cor. 15:35-38, 42-44 NEB)

In what happened at Emmaus and afterwards, an apostolate was commissioned and the future of the Church was assured. Whatever experience these men had of the resurrected Jesus, they lived by it, and in most cases, died for it. It is this reality that undergirds the doctrine of the Resurrection and its centrality in the Christian faith. There is no possibility of recovery of the complete history of what happened. Perhaps if this could be accomplished beyond doubt, there would be no need for faith. But it is by faith in their experience of the risen Christ that the Church, from Emmaus and afterwards, in the words of St. Luke:

'. . . met constantly to hear the apostles teach, and to share the common life, to break bread, and to pray.' (Acts 2:42 NEB)

And so it has continued to our day and will to the end of the age.

This chapter mentioned my own identifying with Paul's experience of the risen and ascended Lord. Can you identify with it, too? Read the experience of Paul as he must have told it to Luke as they traveled together.

Meanwhile Saul was still breathing murderous threats against the disciples of the Lord. He went to the High Priest and applied for letters to the synagogues at Damascus authorizing him to arrest anyone he found, men or women, who followed the new way, and bring them to Jerusalem. While he was still on the road and nearing Damascus, suddenly a light flashed from the sky all around him. He fell to the ground and heard a voice saying, 'Saul, Saul, why do you persecute me?' 'Tell me, Lord,' he said, 'who are you?' The voice answered, 'I am Jesus, whom you are persecuting. But get up and go into the city, and you will be told what you have to do.' Meanwhile the men who were travelling with him stood speechless; they heard the voice but could see no one. Saul got up from the ground, but when he opened his eyes he could not see; so they led him by the hand and brought him into Damascus. He was blind for three days, and took no food or drink.

There was a disciple in Damascus named Ananias. He had a vision in which he heard the voice of the Lord: 'Ananias!' 'Here I am, Lord', he answered. The Lord said to him, 'Go at once to Straight Street, to the house of Judas, and ask for a man from Tarsus named Saul. You will find him at prayer; he has had a vision of a man named Ananias coming in and laying his hands on him to restore his sight.' Ananias answered, 'Lord, I have often heard about this man and all the harm he has done to thy people in Jerusalem. And he is here with authority from the chief priests to arrest all who invoke thy name.' But the Lord said to him, 'You must go, for this man is my chosen instrument to bring my name before the nations and their kings, and before the people of Israel. I myself will show him all that he must go through for my name's sake.'

So Ananias went. He entered the house, laid his hands on him and said, 'Saul, my brother, the Lord Jesus, who appeared to you on your way here, has sent me to you so that you may recover your sight, and be filled with the Holy Spirit.' And immediately it seemed that scales fell from his eyes, and he regained his sight. Thereupon he was baptized, and afterwards he took food and his strength returned.

He stayed some time with the disciples in Damascus. Soon he was proclaiming Jesus publicly in the synagogues: 'This', he said, 'is the Son of God.' (Acts 9:1-20 NEB)

How do you account for Paul's vicious persecution of the Christians? Have you experienced a like resistance in those the Lord is calling? Have you ever seen it in yourself? Does Paul's stubbornness account for the power with which he was confronted? Did the Lord appear only to Paul in this passage? Have you known people in your life who have been given the streaks of light we talk of so much? Has one ever been given to you?

16

Peter the Preacher

An apostle is one sent, literally one "placed in front of" an assembly to give a message. Since we hear so much today about the "lay apostolate," laymen are beginning to get the message that somehow they are related to Peter and the others and are called to do something they don't understand and that no one seems able to explain to them. This chapter may not help much. But I can tell you this, a lay apostle is not so much a person who does something as a person who is a particular someone. He is placed in front of the world by the Lord, a world whose overfriendliness is often harder to deal with than its hostility. An apostle stands there, caught up between the tension of human weakness and Christlikeness striving to affirm in his situation, the Christ in him, rather than deny it. The contrast between Peter the fisherman and Peter the apostle can teach us more about our own apostolate than all the abstract talking around it we can devise.

There is no greater example of the reality that Christ changes men than in the life of St. Peter. The Gospels give us a clear unvarnished account of his character which indicates that he certainly had his share of the weaknesses of humanity, and these were of such a nature as to make him utterly useless for the role Christ had chosen for him.

Perhaps the least of these weaknesses was a kind of impetuosity and lack of judgment that would hardly be a quality one would expect in a future leader of a great enterprise. Here is an example:

> Then he poured water into a basin, and began to wash his disciples' feet and to wipe them with the towel. When it was Simon Peter's turn, Peter said to him, 'You, Lord, washing my feet?' Jesus replied, 'You do not understand now what I am doing, but one day you will.' Peter said, 'I will never let you wash my feet.' 'If I do not wash you,' Jesus replied, 'you are not in fellowship with me.' 'Then, Lord,' said Simon Peter, 'not my feet only; wash my hands and head as well.'
>
> (John 13:5-9 NEB)

and another:

> Then Peter spoke: 'Rabbi,' he said, 'how good it is that we are here! Shall we make three shelters, one for you, one for Moses, and one for Elijah?' (For he did not know what to say; . . .)
>
> (Mark 9:5-7 NEB)

And while, on occasion, he showed flashes of insight:

> 'And you,' he asked, 'who do you say I am?' Simon Peter answered, 'You are the Messiah, the Son of the living God.'
>
> (Matt. 16:16-17 NEB)

he commonly seemed slow to comprehend what Jesus was trying to teach him. For example, this:

> At this, Peter took him by the arm and began to rebuke him: 'Heaven forbid!' he said. 'No, Lord, this shall never happen to you.' Then Jesus turned and said to Peter, 'Away with you, Satan; you are a

stumbling block to me. You think as men think, not as God thinks.'
(Matt. 16:22-23 NEB)

and this:
Then Peter came up and asked, 'Lord, how often am I to forgive my brother if he goes on wronging me? As many as seven times?' Jesus replied, 'I do not say seven times; I say seventy times seven.'
(Matt. 18:21-22 NEB)

In order to understand fully this last, we must remember the oriental use of numbers. Certain numbers, especially three, seven, forty, seventy, a hundred and forty-four, had special significance rather than standing for literal amounts. Peter was probably quite proud of himself and his comprehension of the Lord when he phrased his question because, 'As many as seven times?' was descriptive of his concept of forbearance far beyond the limit of human endurance. Jesus' reply, 'I say seventy times seven,' is an unbelievable number and really means, 'forever.'

Much more disqualifying was Peter's lack of courage. This is nowhere better illustrated than in the account of Peter's denials of Christ. First we have Peter's extravagant claim of undying loyalty:

'Simon, Simon, take heed: Satan has been given leave to sift all of you like wheat; but for you I have prayed that your faith may not fail; and when you have come to yourself, you must lend strength to your brothers.' 'Lord,' he replied, 'I am ready to go with you to prison and death.' Jesus said, 'I tell you, Peter, the cock will not crow tonight until you have three times denied that you know me.'
(Luke 22:31-34 NEB)

and then the three denials:

> Then they arrested him and led him away. They brought him to the High Priest's house, and Peter followed at a distance. They lit a fire in the middle of the courtyard and sat round it, and Peter sat among them. A serving-maid who saw him sitting in the firelight stared at him and said, 'This man was with him too.' But he denied it: 'Woman,' he said, 'I do not know him.' A little later someone else noticed him and said, 'You also are one of them.' But Peter said to him, 'No, I am not.' About an hour passed and another spoke more strongly still: 'Of course this fellow was with him. He must have been; he is a Galilean.' But Peter said, 'Man, I do not know what you are talking about.' At that moment, while he was still speaking, a cock crew; and the Lord turned and looked at Peter.
> (Luke 22:54-60 NEB)

Not only does this incident serve to illustrate Peter's cowardice, but it points out Jesus' plans for him as well. Even more important it prophesies Peter's conversion.

One wonders how these most uncomplimentary incidents, which portray Peter as a blustering braggart and disloyal coward were ever included in Scripture. Certainly none of his fellow Christians who revered him as their leader would have told these things about him. The answer is simple enough. These accounts come from Peter himself. While I have used all four Gospels in compiling these illustrations, all of these incidents are first told in Mark. And while there is considerable disagreement about who Mark is, there is universal agreement that Peter is the source of his material, that he accompanied Peter in his ministry and acted as his secretary, and, on occasion, his interpreter. It is quite natural that Peter would have told these most revealing things about himself in the course of describing his relationship with Jesus and at the same time would have shown the kind of person he was before Jesus changed his life.

If Peter as described in the Gospels represents what he was to begin with, later in the book of Acts is what he became. There are four of Peter's sermons recorded in Acts. These are the earliest remembered sermons of the Church other than those of Jesus. The sermons themselves much predate Luke's writing them down in their present form, and many scholars believe that they were part of a collection that Luke used in compiling the Acts of the Apostles, which is a sequel to his Gospel.

The content of these sermons follows a pattern which has come to be called by scholars the *Kerygma*. This is derived from the Greek word *Keryx*, which means a herald. The Kerygma is that which the herald proclaims. I mention this name for the pattern of the proclamation of the gospel by the early Church because the word is widely used in commentaries on Scripture and if you happen to do further reading on the New Testament you will undoubtedly find it aggravatingly untranslated and unexplained. The general pattern of the Kerygma is this:

1. The proclamation that the time foretold in the prophets has been fulfilled.

2. This fulfillment has taken place in the life, ministry, death and Resurrection of Jesus Christ. Specific prophecies are cited to show that this has happened.

3. In his Resurrection from the dead, Jesus is proclaimed as the Messiah and ruler of Israel.

4. The presence of the Holy Spirit in the Church is the manifestation of the power of Christ.

5. The Messianic Age will shortly reach its con-

summation in the second coming of Christ.

6. These sermons commonly close with an exhortation to repent, which will bring forgiveness of sins, the gift of the Holy Spirit and the promise of salvation.*

The first sermon of Peter which will be recorded below is one of the finest examples of the Kerygma. While it cannot be definitely established that this sermon is couched in the very language of Peter, we can be sure that its content would reflect his method of proclaiming the gospel.

But Peter stood up with the Eleven, raised his voice, and addressed them: 'Fellow Jews, and all you who live in Jerusalem, mark this and give me a hearing. These men are not drunk, as you imagine; for it is only nine in the morning. No, this is what the prophet spoke of: "God says, 'This will happen in the last days: I will pour out upon everyone a portion of my spirit, and your sons and daughters shall prophesy; your young men shall see visions, and your old men shall dream dreams. Yes, I will endue even my slaves, both men and women, with a portion of my spirit, and they shall prophesy. And I will show portents in the sky above, and signs on the earth below—blood and fire and drifting smoke. The sun shall be turned to darkness, and the moon to blood, before that great, resplendent day, the day of the Lord, shall come. And then, everyone who invokes the name of the Lord shall be saved.'"

'Men of Israel, listen to me: I speak of Jesus of

---

*This pattern of the Kerygma is adapted freely from the work of Alan Richardson, *AN INTRODUCTION TO THE THEOLOGY OF THE NEW TESTAMENT*, Harper & Row, New York, 1958, which also reflects the original work done by C.H. Dodd in England.

Nazareth, a man singled out by God and made known to you through miracles, portents, and signs, which God worked among you through him, as you well know. When he had been given up to you, by the deliberate will and plan of God, you used heathen men to crucify and kill him. But God raised him to life again setting him free from the pangs of death, because it could not be that death should keep him in his grip.

For David says of him:

"I foresaw that the presence of the Lord
    would be with me always,
for he is at my right hand
    so that I may not be shaken;
therefore my heart was glad
    and my tongue spoke my joy;
moreover, my flesh shall dwell in hope,
for thou wilt not abandon my soul to death,
nor let thy loyal servant suffer corruption.
Thou hast shown me the ways of life,
thou wilt fill me with gladness by thy presence."

'Let me tell you plainly, my friends, that the patriarch David died and was buried, and his tomb is here to this very day. It is clear therefore that he spoke as a prophet, who knew that God had sworn to him that one of his own direct descendants should sit on his throne; and when he said he was not abandoned to death, and his flesh never suffered corruption, he spoke with foreknowledge of the resurrection of the Messiah. The Jesus we speak of has been raised by God, as we can all bear witness. Exalted thus with God's right hand, he received the Holy Spirit from the Father, as was promised, and all that you now see and hear flows from him. For it was not David who went up to heaven; his own words are: "The Lord said to my Lord, 'Sit at my right hand until I make your enemies your footstool.' " Let all Israel then accept as certain that God has made this Jesus, whom you crucified, both Lord and Messiah.'

When they heard this they were cut to the heart, and said to Peter and the apostles, 'Friends, what are we to do?' 'Repent,' said Peter, 'repent and be baptized, every one of you, in the name of Jesus the Messiah for the forgiveness of your sins; and you will receive the gift of the Holy Spirit. For the promise is to you, and your children, and to all who are far away, every one whom the Lord our God may call.'

In these and many other words he pressed his case and pleaded with them: 'Save yourselves,' he said, 'from this crooked age.' Then those who accepted his word were baptized, and some three thousand were added to their number that day.
(Acts 2:14-41 NEB)

Not every example of the Kerygma contains each of the six parts mentioned above. There is no reference in this particular sermon to the second coming. However, the other five parts follow the pattern very well.

Imagine the circumstances surrounding this particular sermon. Jesus has already lost His life by a criminal execution on the basis of His Messianic claims and the threat they leveled at the Jewish religious establishment. Peter goes into the same situation boldly and speaks with great force and courage among these very people. Notice the language he uses in accusing them.

When he had been given up to you, by the deliberate will and plan of God, you used heathen men to crucify and kill him.

This is not the kind of expression we would expect from the cowardly Peter of the Gospels. He was quite aware of the risks he was running by his outspokenness, but he continued to fly in the face of danger again and again.

> The God of Abraham, Isaac, and Jacob, the God of our fathers, has given the highest honour to his servant Jesus, whom you committed for trial and repudiated in Pilate's court—repudiated the one who was holy and righteous when Pilate had decided to release him. You begged as a favor the release of a murderer, and killed him who has led the way to life. But God raised him from the dead; of that we are witnesses.
> (Acts 3:13-15 NEB)

This particular accusation, accompanied as it was by a healing miracle, caused Peter and the apostles to be hailed into court.

'By what power,' they asked, 'or by what name have such men as you done this?' Then Peter, filled with the Holy Spirit, answered, 'Rulers of the people and elders, if the question put to us today is about help given to a sick man, and we are asked by what means he was cured, here is the answer, for all of you and for all the people of Israel: It was by the name of Jesus Christ of Nazareth, whom you crucified, whom God has raised from the dead; it is by his name that this man stands before you fit and well.
(Acts 4:7-10 NEB)

This left the court in a difficult situation. The man was indeed well and there was no way they could discredit Peter and the apostles before the people. So they sent them away, conferred together and then brought them back privately.

They then called them in and ordered them to refrain from all public speaking and teaching in the name of Jesus.

But Peter and John said to them in reply: 'Is it right in God's eyes for us to obey you rather than God? Judge for yourselves. We cannot possibly give up speaking of things we have seen and heard.'
(Acts 4:18-20 NEB)

Peter continued in his bold leadership of the apostles, refusing to keep silent, in spite of other arrests, flogging and prison. And so he lived the remainder of his life, proclaiming the good news in Jerusalem and finally in Rome, where he met his death, courageous at the end, insisting, according to tradition, that he be crucified upside down because he was unworthy to die in the way that Jesus did.

While the Kerygma was the common proclamation of the primitive Church, there is strong evidence, other than that its earliest examples were attributed to him, that Peter was the author and developer of the pattern. The first epistle of Peter supports this claim. While he was writing to those already converted and faithful, all the elements of the Kerygma are present and well developed in this letter. You may want to read through the epistle picking out the passages which conform to the six points of the Kerygma pattern. In the first chapter there are the first five well defined.

1. This salvation was the theme which the prophets pondered and explored, those who prophesied the grace of God awaiting you.
(1 Pet. 1:10 NEB)

2. Praise be to the God and Father of our Lord Jesus Christ, who in his great mercy gave us new

birth into a living hope by the resurrection of Jesus Christ from the dead!

(1 Pet. 1:3 NEB)

3. Through him you have come to trust in God who raised him from the dead and *gave him glory*, so that your faith and hope are fixed on God.

(1 Pet. 1:21 NEB, italics mine)

4. And now it has been openly announced to you through preachers who brought you the Gospel in the power of the Holy Spirit sent from heaven.

(1 Pet. 1:12 NEB)

5. Fix your hopes on the gift of grace which is to be yours when Jesus Christ is revealed.

(1 Pet. 1:13 NEB)

This is by no means an exhaustive compilation. Almost every verse, in one way or another, presents this primitive pattern of the proclamation of the gospel. But what of the sixth point in the pattern, the exhortation to repentance? Remember that this was written for the faithful, who had presumably already repented and made their peace with God. In sermons preached to those already in the Church a new kind of preaching developed which has its own Greek name, *Didache*, which means teaching. Our word didactic is cognate with it. So what would correspond to exhortation to repentance in preaching directed to the unconverted becomes instruction in how to behave for the faithful. The structure of the preaching and writing, common in Paul's letters as well as in this one of Peter, is in two major parts: The Kerygma, or proclamation of God's action in saving man through Jesus Christ, followed by the Didache, or therefore, this is how you should behave. The Didache section of this letter from Peter is very evident, beginning:

Dear friends, I beg you, as aliens in a foreign

land, to abstain from the lusts of the flesh which are at war with the soul.

(1 Pet. 2:11 NEB)

So this remarkable letter, written by a man who was converted from a bumbling weakling to a tower of strength, strongly resembles in its content the earliest recorded Christian sermons as preserved in the book of Acts. It seems quite clear to me that they are products of the same mind.

It is noteworthy that this letter, known as the epistle of courage, was written to a group of Christians under persecution. The strengthening faith that altered the life of Peter is not anywhere more evident than in this epistle, especially in these verses:

For it is a fine thing if a man endure the pain of undeserved suffering because God is in his thoughts. What credit is there in fortitude when you have done wrong and are beaten for it? But when you have behaved well and suffer for it, your fortitude is a fine thing in the sight of God.

(1 Pet. 2:19-20 NEB)

Remembering that Christ endured bodily suffering, you must arm yourselves with a temper of mind like his. When a man has thus endured bodily suffering he has finished with sin, and for the rest of his days on earth he may live, not for the things men desire, but for what God wills.

(1 Pet. 4:1-2 NEB)

An even more important work, with far-reaching consequences, bears witness to the part Peter had in the formulation of the Kerygma. This is the Gospel according to St. Mark. We have already said that Peter's preaching and reminiscences are the foundation of this Gospel. When we read it we are struck by the fact that it is pure proclamation of God's action in saving men through Jesus Christ. A careful reading with this fact in mind will show how completely Peter's thought and witness is embodied in this Gospel. From the beginning: "Here begins the Gospel of Jesus Christ the Son of God" (Mark 1:1 NEB), to the end:

> So after talking with them the Lord Jesus was taken up into heaven, and he took his seat at the right hand of God; but they went out to make their proclamation everywhere, and the Lord worked with them and confirmed their words by the miracles that followed.
>
> (Mark 16:19-20 NEB)

And there it is. Peter the blusterer became Peter the preacher. What made the transformation? Certainly it was that gigantic streak of light that came upon Peter as he saw the resurrected Lord that enabled him to get it all together. What Jesus saw existing potentially in Peter the risen Christ brought into actuality. After the Apostolic Age, men were not given the experience of seeing their risen Lord through their visual senses but, through the awareness given by the persistent and courageous proclamations of Peter the preacher and his successors, men and women in our day experience the power of the Holy Spirit in their lives.

Each of us who profess and call ourselves Christians have an apostolate. Before we can exercise it we must be sent. What we are sent to depends on what God has made us to be. It happens He made me to be a priest and my life consists of becoming—despite the many pockets of resistance in me—what God has made me to be. But all too often lay people perceive they are "ones sent" and head for the most convenient seminary. The notion that the only way to fulfill an apostolate is to be ordained has produced more clergymen than the

Church can afford. God takes you as you are and makes you what He intends you to be. Whether you are ordained or not has nothing to do with it. Being what you are intended to be, affirming Christ in you has everything to do with it.

When I call Peter the preacher in this chapter I do not define preaching as mounting a pulpit or gathering a crowd at a street corner and haranguing them. But everyone sent is to publish the Kerygma, to be a living proclamation of the good news, a victor over human weakness and a manifestation of Christ as He lives in you. Out of this process comes a knowledge of what to do.

Consider this:

I entreat you, then—I, a prisoner for the Lord's sake: as God has called you, live up to your calling. Be humble always and gentle, and patient too. Be forbearing with one another and charitable. Spare no effort to make fast with bonds of peace the unity which the Spirit gives. There is one body and one Spirit, as there is also one hope held out in God's call to you; one Lord, one faith, one baptism; one God and Father of all, who is over all and through all and in all.

But each of us has been given his gift, his due portion of Christ's bounty. Therefore Scripture says:

'He ascended into the heights with captives in his train; he gave gifts to men.'

Now, the word 'ascended' implies that he also descended to the lowest level, down to the very earth. He who descended is no other than he who ascended far above all heavens, so that he might fill the universe. And these were his gifts: some to be apostles, some prophets, some evangelists, some pastors and teachers, to equip God's people for work in his service, to the building up of the body of Christ. So shall we all at last attain to the unity inherent in our faith and our knowledge of the Son of God—to mature manhood, measured by nothing less than the full stature of Christ. We are no longer to be children, tossed by the waves and whirled about by every fresh gust of teaching, dupes of crafty rogues and their deceitful schemes. No, let us speak the truth in love, so shall we fully grow up into Christ. He is the head, and on him the whole body depends. Bonded and knit together by every constituent joint, the whole frame grows through the due activity of each part, and builds itself up in love.

(Eph. 4:1-16 NEB)

In the first of this exposition of God's call, what does He call you to be? Read between the lines—listing what is explicit is not enough. What is implicit? Does this apply only to those in Holy Orders? What is the basic quality of the gift we possess? Does the list of gifts exhaust the possibilities? What do these gifts develop in us? What is our ultimate achievement? The ultimate character of the Church?

17

Saint Paul and the Football Coach

This book has been made up of a parade of men illumined by the streaks of light God used to communicate with them: among them Abraham, Moses, the prophets, Job, the Jahwist, Peter and Paul, all of them contributing to the word of God, lighting our way. "Your word is a lantern to my feet and a light upon my path" (Ps. 119:105 PBCP). The light points the way to the word, to Jesus the Christ. In this chapter I want to show the power of Paul to lead to Christ, to show how the light he shed on the pathway has endured twenty centuries to inspire a much admired and respected person in the contemporary sports world. But even more, I want to show the light Paul furnishes us as we strive to find the way.

We have elsewhere mentioned the conversion of Paul from a zealous persecutor of the followers of Christ to an even more zealous proponent of Christianity. However, it is important to examine Paul's motives, as a Pharisee, for his fanatic destruction of the Church in order to understand better his function within the Church after he became a part of it. As a well trained and sophisticated Pharisee, he believed that Jesus' death on the cross, a death that made him accursed in the eyes of the law, would completely discredit him with the Jews, and so at first he may well have followed the advice of his teacher, Gamaliel:

> Men of Israel, be cautious in deciding what to do with these men. Some time ago Theudas came forward, claiming to be somebody, and a number of men, about four hundred, joined him. But he was killed and his whole following was broken up and disappeared. After him came Judas the Galilean at the time of the census; he induced some people to revolt under his leadership, but he too perished and his whole following was scattered. And so now: keep clear of these men, I tell you; leave them alone. For if this idea of theirs or its execution is of human origin, it will collapse; but if it is from God, you will never be able to put them down, and you risk finding yourselves at war with God.
> (Acts 5:35-39 NEB)

However, as the following of the apostles grew at an alarming rate, Paul, (or Saul as he was called in Hebrew) saw the threat in the teaching of the Christians to the sanctity of the law and felt called to fight it with all his strength. He was a party to the martyrdom of Stephen. He hunted down and harried the Church in Jerusalem, and then he received official permission to carry his harassment on to Damascus, hoping to destroy the burgeoning Church there. It was on this journey that the risen Christ appeared to Paul and called him to his ministry. There are three accounts of this appearance in the book of Acts and one hint of it from Paul's own pen in the first letter to Corinth (1 Cor. 15:1-8). He also makes allusion to it in the epistle to the Galatians (Gal. 1:16). It is obvious that there could be only one source for all these accounts. Only Paul himself could tell what happened on the road to Damascus, how his fierce pride in his sense of dedication to the God of his fathers was shattered by his encounter with Jesus, his ego was surrendered to his Lord. It was this appearance that changed everything for Paul. He saw now that Jesus was indeed raised from the dead as the apostles claimed. Therefore, rather than being an executed revolutionary He was the Messiah of God.

Paul was the most highly educated and sophisticated of the apostles. He had grown up in Tarsus, a center of Greek culture, which, though not of the same magnitude of Alexandria in Egypt, was well known. Not only was Paul trained in his own religious heritage by the best teaching available, but he was also well versed in the philosophy of the Greeks. Moreover, he was gifted with an intensity of soul and keenness of mind that suited him admirably for the work to which his Lord had called him. From tradition we gather that he was not a prepossessing person in appearance—he was short of stature, and swarthy. He was also given to bluntness which bordered on tactlessness and frequently infuriated his hearers so that he often found himself in trouble. But he had a way of winning in the end.

After his initial visit to Damascus and brief fellowship with Ananias, he went into the solitude of the desert to think through the implications of the Lord's appearance to him. Here it was that he realized the truth in Jesus' teaching; that no man could get into right relationship with God through the keeping of the law, that the keeping of the whole law was an impossibility. Either the attempt would condemn a man to an endless bondage to guilt or he would escape into petty concerns over the trivia of the law, which, while it diverted a man from self-condemnation, he became so enslaved by detail that he missed involvement in the truly important concerns. Beginning in this period the streaks of light came that opened his eyes to the meaning of the life, death and Resurrection of Jesus Christ. Slowly he fitted the Christ event into the detailed knowledge he had of the Old Testament. After a suitable period of listening, he was ready to obey.

In order to understand the controversy which surrounded Paul's ministry, it is necessary to realize that Christianity began as a small sect in Judaism. The controversy between the members of this sect and those who did not accept Jesus as the Messiah centered not so much on the claims of Messiahship as in the attitude of Christians toward the Law. It was the concept of freedom in Christ which threatened the traditions of Judaism and caused the trouble between Christian and non-Christian Jews. There was a conservative element within the Christian Church that insisted on the keeping of the law, especially in regard to the circumcision of Gentile converts (which in those days of primitive knowledge of sanitation could amount to a death sentence for a grown man), and in connection with the regulations requiring that Jews could not eat with Gentiles. It is easy to see the threat of the latter concept to the celebration of the Holy Communion within a Christian congregation of mixed origins. The reason for this conservatism was not so much, it would seem to me, based on the principle that the Jewish law ought to be incorporated into Christianity, as it was urged as a matter of expediency.

By obeying especially these two key precepts, the Christian congregations removed their threats to Judaism and thereby placated the Jewish congregations and avoided persecution by them. Paul, however, saw that by acting contrary to the principles of

Christian freedom set forth in the new covenant, or promised redemption through the Messiah and establishment of the new Israel as superseding the old, the whole message of the gospel was lost and the power of the cross destroyed. Whether Paul carried his point through the power of his own insistence or whether the overwhelming number of Gentile converts by that time forced the issue, the matter was settled at a council held in Jerusalem about 49 A.D. Luke records it thus:

> We, the apostles and elders, send greetings as brothers to our brothers of gentile origin in Antioch, Syria and Cilicia. Forasmuch as we have heard that some of our number, without any instructions from us, have disturbed you with their talk and unsettled your minds, we have resolved . . . to send to you our chosen representatives with our well-beloved Barnabas and Paul, who have devoted themselves to the cause of our Lord Jesus Christ. We are therefore sending Judas and Silas, who will themselves confirm this by word of mouth. It is the decision of the Holy Spirit, and our decision, to lay no further burden upon you beyond these essentials: You are to abstain from meat that has been offered to idols, from blood, from anything that has been strangled, and from fornication.
>
> If you keep yourselves free from these things you will be doing right. Farewell.
>
> (Acts 15:23-29 NEB)

Such was the declaration of the council, recorded for us some forty years after it took place. Paul has a version of some of the behind the scenes conversation, recorded perhaps in the same year it occurred.

> But as for the men of high reputation (not that their importance matters to me: God does not

recognize these personal distinctions) these men of repute, I say, did not prolong the consultation, but on the contrary acknowledged that I had been entrusted with the Gospel for the Gentiles as surely as Peter had been entrusted with the Gospel for Jews. For God whose action made Peter an apostle to the Jews, also made me an apostle to the Gentiles.

Recognizing, then, the favor thus bestowed upon me, those reputed pillars of our society, James, Cephas, and John, accepted Barnabas and myself as partners, and shook hands upon it, agreeing that we should go to the Gentiles while they went to the Jews. All they asked was that we should keep their poor in mind, which was the very thing I made it my business to do.

(Gal. 2:6-10 NEB)

Thus the first of many splits in the Church was settled. However, as is often the case, it was a long time before the wounds were completely healed. The letter to Galatia, written after the council, since the action of the council is referred to in it, as indicated by the quotation above, is written to counteract the effect of the Judaizing Christians upon this young group of churches. This letter is worthy of careful study, because it not only records the nature of this controversy, but also makes an initial expression of the doctrine of coming into a right relationship with God through faith in Jesus Christ. This doctrine is called "justification by faith" by theologians, and it is set forth in Galatians, and later, in a more mature manner, in Romans. It was the doctrine that became the cornerstone in Martin Luther's theology. In addition, this letter contains a very clear expression of the relationship between the law and grace as understood in the Christian faith.

No one can hope to do any kind of justice to St. Paul in a single chapter. I only hope I can arouse your interest enough that you will read these letters Paul wrote. This is not an easy task. Bear in mind that these are letters written by Paul to deal with situations which came up in the churches he founded. He had no notion that he was writing what would eventually be revered as holy Scripture. Moreover, these letters, usually dictated to a professional secretary, were often written in haste, as Paul was much more interested in founding new churches than in taking care of those he had founded. It is not that he didn't care for all the churches. His letters are full of love. But there is evidence of a hurried kind of composition as indicated in the example below. Here he is addressing himself to a quarrel within the church at Corinth where factions had grown up on the basis of loyalty to the particular minister who brought them into the church.

I have been told, my brothers, by Chloe's people that there are quarrels among you. What I mean is this: each of you is saying, 'I am Paul's man', or 'I am for Apollos'; 'I follow Cephas', or 'I am Christ's.' Surely Christ has not been divided among you! Was it Paul who was crucified for you? Was it in the name of Paul that you were baptized? Thank God, I never baptized one of you— except Crispus and Gaius. So no one can say you were baptized in my name. Yes, I did baptize the household of Stephanas; I cannot think of anyone else.

(1 Cor. 1:11-16 NEB)

As one who is quite accustomed to dictating correspondence and one who is chronically in a hurry, I recognize the symptoms of both these problems in this passage. Notice the headlong way in which the phrases tumble out, Paul's mind eager to get on, so that he forgets whom he has baptized, and then, as his memory corrects him, he adds the household of Stephanas as an afterthought. It all makes for a vivid revelation of Paul's personality, but sometimes, when he is dealing with profound theological concepts, and his mind goes racing ahead of his mouth, it produces difficult reading. The magnitude of the concepts he is dealing with sometimes demands more careful composition than he is willing to give, but the power and force of his personality make up for the occasional lack of clarity.

The two letters to the Corinthians are good ones to read first because they cover, between them, the range of Paul's moods. But in order to understand what you are reading you have to realize that these are fragments of four letters, most probably, rather than two. The recipients of Paul's letters did not always realize their value, and when the letters began to be collected and copied a generation later, parts had been lost and pages were out of order or scrolls were torn and mended. So now we have to reconstruct them as best we can. Below is the simplest and most common reconstruction.

First Letter:
2 Corinthians 6:14-7:1
It is obvious that this is just a fragment and that the rest of this letter is lost. However, reference is made to it in 1 Corinthians 5:9: "In my letter I wrote you to have nothing to do with loose livers." This small section in 2 Corinthians seems to have nothing to do with what goes before or follows it and therefore must be part of this first letter that has been misplaced. Presumably the rest of the letter is lost.

Second Letter
1 Corinthians

While agreement is not universal, it is generally accepted that this letter, with minor exception, is a single letter and complete. While Paul rebukes the congregation at Corinth for a number of things, the letter contains some of the most sublime of Paul's writing, especially, the 13th and the 15th chapters. One would think the Corinthians would receive this beautiful letter well but they did not and from the tone of the third letter, their reply must have been a most uncomplimentary attempt to discredit Paul's apostleship and his authority over them.

Third Letter
2 Corinthians 10-13

Paul is hurt and angry at the rebellious Corinthians and lets them know it in no uncertain terms. This, too, is fragmentary, but we seem to have the last part of the letter. Apparently the vehemence and power of Paul got to the Corinthians and their reply must have indicated repentance and a desire for reconciliation.

Fourth Letter
2 Corinthians 1-9 less 6:14-7:1

This is a beautiful letter of love and reconciliation.

Try reading these letters in this order, preferably in the New English Bible, and see if they aren't much clearer.

I leave you to discover the rest of Paul's epistles for yourself. Those generally considered by scholars as directly written by Paul are Romans, 1 and 2 Corinthians, Galatians, Philippians, Colossians, 1 and

2 Thessalonians, and Philemon. 1 and 2 Timothy and Titus, called the pastoral epistles, may be put together with genuine fragments of Paul's letters that have been heavily edited. Ephesians seems to be a composition which may have served as a covering letter for a collection of the genuine epistles, and which summarizes Paul's theology but is not in the style and not always in the language of Paul. But the author, whoever he was, was steeped in the theology of Paul and makes an admirable summary of most of his teaching.

But the effect of Paul's ministry to the Gentile Church did not end when his voice was stilled by the hand of the persecutors of the Church. Wherever Christian congregations have assembled to worship, his words have been heard for century after century, and the lives of men have been changed and influenced by them. This chapter promises in its title to suggest some kind of relationship between St. Paul and a football coach. And so there was.

The late Vince Lombardi, the coach who led the Green Bay Packers to a series of championships, was a devout Roman Catholic who habitually attended daily Mass. The epistle, (or letter) perhaps not always from Paul, is an invariable feature of the Mass, and since most of the epistles were written by Paul or influenced by him, there is abundant evidence of the saint's influence on the football coach. Jerry Kramer's two books on his career with the Packers quote Lombardi many times, and quite often the basis of the thought behind the quotes can be traced back to St. Paul. One example will suffice:

". . . a few weeks later, before the game for the Western Conference title, he [Lombardi] quoted passionately from one of St. Paul's epistles and really fired us up."*

---

*Farewell to Football, Page 29.

It does not take much knowledge of Coach Lombardi to know which passage he quoted:

> You know (do you not?) that at the sports all the runners run the race, though only one wins the prize. Like them, run to win! But every athlete goes into strict training. They do it to win a fading wreath; we, a wreath that never fades. For my part, I run with a clear goal before me; I am like a boxer who does not beat the air; I bruise my own body and make it know its master, for fear that after preaching to others I should find myself rejected.
>
> (1 Cor. 9:24-27 NEB)

But the real test of influence is whether he who influences you becomes part of the fiber of your being. The theology of Paul became so much a part of Coach Lombardi that even though one might not be able to attribute the things he said or wrote directly to passages from St. Paul, yet the mark of Paul's thinking is abundantly evident. Vince Lombardi was called upon to write the foreword for Phil Pepe's book, *Winners Never Quit*. What he wrote, which will be quoted below is one of the finest contemporary expressions of the Pauline theology of the stewardship of life I have ever seen.

> This is a book about men in sports, men who through discipline and sacrifice overcame adversity to join the company of champions. It is a book I welcome, for too often today success in anything is attributed solely to talent. Talent is the obvious ingredient of greatness. As will be apparent, however, to the reader who follows here the careers of Mickey Mantle, Sandy Koufax, Johnny Unitas, Jerry Kramer and the others, talent alone could not have won for them their places of honor

in the history of sports and in the hearts of its followers. The hidden ingredients that nurtured the roots of their talent and on which it flourished were determination and dedication.

Talent is a gift, but it is more than that. It is a trust which no man has a right to ignore or, worse still, abuse. Each man, whatever the degree of talent bestowed upon him, has a moral responsibility, not only to himself but to society, to develop that gift to its utmost degree. The men whose stories are recorded in this book are men who, in their Spartan approach to life and to their sport, met this responsibility. They had the courage and the determination—the mental toughness—not only to succeed for themselves but, in the examples they set, to succeed for all men. Not only they but all of us are the better for it.

Vince Lombardi

Coach Lombardi, through his faith and devotion to Christ, his attentiveness to St. Paul and the power of the Holy Spirit, took the insights Paul gave him and applied them to his own apostolate. This is precisely what I meant in the early part of the book when I alluded to the reality that the more our mind-set is like that of those who lived in faith and expectance that God would communicate with them, the more He would communicate with us in our own day and age. Coach Lombardi exemplifies this to me. Even one ignorant of the sports world but who knows the Lord realizes that "Each man, whatever the degree of talent bestowed upon him, has a moral responsibility not only to himself, but to society to develop that gift to the utmost degree"; or "When a lamp is lit, it is not put under the meal-tub, but on the lampstand, where it gives light to everyone in the house" (Matt. 5:15 NEB).

Discussion Guide

We have talked about the lay apostolate in the previous chapter; in this we have met one of its members. In the last discussion guide we meditated on a call. In this we will meditate on the obedience required for response.

Therefore, my brothers, I implore you by God's mercy to offer your very selves to him: a living sacrifice, dedicated and fit for his acceptance, the worship offered by mind and heart. Adapt yourselves no longer to the pattern of this present world, but let your minds be remade and your whole nature thus transformed. Then you will be able to discern the will of God, and to know what is good, acceptable, and perfect.

In virtue of the gift that God in his grace has given me I say to everyone among you: do not be conceited or think too highly of yourself; but think your way to a sober estimate based on the measure of faith that God has dealt to each of you. For just as in a single human body there are many limbs and organs, all with different functions, so all of us, united with Christ, form one body, serving individually as limbs and organs to one another.

The gifts we possess differ as they are allotted to us by God's grace, and must be exercised accordingly: the gift of inspired utterance, for example, in proportion to a man's faith; or the gift of administration, in administration. A teacher should employ his gift in teaching, and one who has the gift of stirring speech should use it to stir his hearers. If you give to charity, give with all your heart; if you are a leader, exert yourself to lead; if you are helping others in distress, do it cheerfully.

Love in all sincerity, loathing evil and clinging

to the good. Let love for our brotherhood breed warmth of mutual affection. Give pride of place to one another in esteem.

With unflagging energy, in ardour of spirit, serve the Lord.

Let hope keep you joyful; in trouble stand firm; persist in prayer.

Contribute to the needs of God's people, and practise hospitality.

Call down blessings on your persecutors—blessings, not curses.

With the joyful be joyful, and mourn with the mourners.

Care as much about each other as about yourselves. Do not be haughty, but go about with humble folk. Do not keep thinking how wise you are.

Never pay back evil for evil. Let your aims be such as all men count honourable. If possible, so far as it lies with you, live at peace with all men. My dear friends, do not seek revenge, but leave a place for divine retribution; for there is a text which reads: 'Justice is mine, says the Lord, I will repay.' But there is another text: 'If your enemy is hungry, feed him; if he is thirsty, give him a drink; by doing this you will heap live coals on his head.' Do not let evil conquer you, but use good to defeat evil.

Rom. 12:1-21 (NEB)

What must we do first? What kind of offering does God want? (Again, read between the lines, don't just give back what the text says.) What does this enable us to be? (Two things.) How do we work together? Do you find your gift listed? Is this list meant to be all inclusive? How do you stack up on the list of things to do? Where are you weak? Where are you strong? Where else do we hear the exhortations in verses 17-21? What is the key for obeying them?

18

A Glimpse into Heaven

The Bible is meant for us as an experience in the depth of being, an experience often grasped fleetingly and intuitively rather than consciously and cognitively. In a lecture I heard recently, Dr. Bernard Meland said, "We live more deeply than we can think." This certainly applies to our living with God through the Bible (and however else we do it) and is epitomized in the Revelation of St. John the Divine. While this final chapter is an attempt to help you make some intellectual sense of the Revelation and enable you to understand why it is written the way it is, it will not enable you to appreciate it. That comes, not as something that can be given you by someone else, but as a fruit of the Spirit that grows in you. This fruit is nurtured and cultivated by the experience of God in your life! By this means you are to perceive and appreciate in your inward self the glimpse into heaven John offers us.

There is nothing so confusing to the person in the pew attempting to make sense out of the Bible as his entering into the Revelation of John. Usually, after a very brief excursion, the reader retreats in perplexity and gives it up. Nor is this confusion confined to the amateur. Because of the very nature of the literary form of this work, much of its original significance and meaning is lost forever and can only be reconstructed in a very tentative way. This is not to say that the book has no value for us or that we should not concern ourselves with it. Used properly, there are beautiful and meaningful parts of it that enrich greatly the New Testament. However, involving oneself in great mathematical calculations and trying to discover the day of the world's end thereby is not a proper or even possible use of this book. History is dotted with groups and sects, who, after intense study of Daniel and the Revelation (the *apocalypses* of the Bible), have come up with a date for the world's end and have dressed themselves in white nightgowns and have gone to a mountaintop to wait, only to have the day come and go with nothing happening.

The Revelation is a literal translation of the Greek word apocalypse, which refers to the literary form in which this book is written. The apocalypse is a distinctive Semitic form of writing which has no counterpart in our culture. However, by understanding this particular device we can find meaning in this work, and what is more important, we can discern which passages cannot be understood in our day.

Below are the general characteristics of apocalyptic writing. Not all of these apply to the Revelation of John, but they do give us useful insights into the book and the way it has been understood.

An apocalypse:
1. Is written as a message of hope to the faithful in a time of persecution.
2. Refers to situations in contemporary history in symbolic and fantastic language understood by the sufferers but not by the persecutors. (Nor always by those in succeeding generations.)
3. Generally describes a cosmic struggle between

good and evil forces of which the intended readers are the victims.
4. Promises eventual deliverance by the forces of good in an age which is soon to come. (This is not to be confused with the kind of ethical kingdom of heaven that Jesus taught, in which the phrases "Thy kingdom come" and "Thy will be done" are interchangeable. When God's will is done, his kingdom will have come.) The apocalyptic age to come is a completely new creation; heaven brought down to earth. You might as well learn the word "eschatology" if you haven't already made its acquaintance. It refers to the last things: death, judgment, heaven and hell, and by extension to this kind of apocalyptic age to come.
5. Is usually written in the name of an ancient worthy: Moses, Enoch, Daniel. However, John does not identify himself as the apostle John, and since he simply says his name is John, a name almost as common in the first century as it is now, we can assume he used his own name. However, the Church has expected the name of some important figure, and therefore has sometimes identified the John of the Revelation with the John of the Gospel.

Previously we talked about the structure of the Bible: that chapters 1 through 11 of Genesis are the prologue, explaining the predicament of man and how he finds himself in it; the remainder of Genesis is the setting, showing God's choice of a people to be the instrument of a particular kind of revelation; and the whole of the Bible from Exodus through the Revelation is the saga of God's redemption of mankind. We arrive now at the end of the book, and the action goes on. We see God's use of the form of the apocalypse, not only to strengthen his people, tempted to apostasy under persecution, but much more importantly, to allow them a glimpse of their ultimate destiny—the fruit of their redemption—in an ethereal and poetic manner. In this we begin to intuit what it all means.

The most probable time for this to have been written would have been toward the end of the reign of Domitian who was the emperor of Rome until 96 A.D. Domitian insisted that he be worshiped as a god in a somewhat more arrogant way than some of his predecessors, probably because he was far from godlike. For some generations the Jews were exempted from emperor worship because of their adamant refusal to participate in it, no matter what, and also because the Romans looked upon them as a somewhat strange and troublesome people, and decided it was politic to humor them. The Christians shared in this exemption largely until the reign of Domitian, but by that time the Gentile Christians were much in the majority, and Christianity had developed the character of a separate religion. Under Domitian the punishment for refusal to worship Caesar because of Christian scruples was severe flogging, torture, even banishment, but it was not fatal as it came to be later on. John had apparently been exiled on the island of Patmos as his sentence for refusing to take part in emperor worship. There were some apostate (or "turncoat") Christians in this persecution and John wrote to strengthen the Christian community against the danger of defection.

By this time there was probably some circulation of Paul's letters in a single volume, and there is some evidence that John was acquainted with them. His letters, then, to the seven churches is probably a literary device in imitation of the actual letters of Paul, rather than letters to each of the seven churches. The ascriptions to these churches, which take up the first three chapters, are interesting depictions of the shortcomings to Christian churches, but not of any great value. Much of the meaning of certain of the specific allusions has been lost.

Because the bulk of this book is a vision of heaven, its value and proper use is liturgical rather than for literal basis for doctrine. That is, the beauty and power of the language is suited best to the expression of worship. In the churches who use a formal liturgical worship, passages from the Revelation take the place of the epistle on at least three of the major holy days of the church calendar. Among these is the feast of St. Michael and All Angels, much more celebrated in England then here.

I want to quote from the portion of Scripture appointed for the epistle for St. Michael's, which is an expression, in Christian mythological terms, of the struggle between good and evil, characteristic of apocalyptical writing.

> Then war broke out in heaven. Michael and his angels waged war upon the dragon. The dragon and his angels fought, but they had not the strength to win, and no foothold was left them in heaven. So the great dragon was thrown down, that serpent of old that led the whole world astray, whose name is Satan, or the Devil—thrown down to the earth, and his angels with him.
>
> Then I heard a voice in heaven proclaiming aloud: 'This is the hour of victory for our God, the hour of his sovereignty and power, when his Christ comes to his rightful rule! For the accuser of our brothers is overthrown, who day and night accused them before our God. By the sacrifice of the Lamb they have conquered him, and by the testimony which they uttered; for they did not hold their lives too dear to lay them down. Rejoice

then, you heavens and you that dwell in them! But woe to you, earth and sea, for the Devil has come down to you in great fury, knowing that his time is short!'

(Rev. 12:7-12 NEB)

We first meet the devil face to face in this book in the chapter called "The Impertinence of Job" and we continue to encounter him until finally he does his worst in the "Three Long Hours." Here we have, expressed in poetic terms, the overcoming of the devil in a cosmic struggle that we have expressed in terms of human history on a dismal Friday afternoon on the cross.

It is easy to see that this kind of reminder of the cosmic struggle between the forces of good and evil would serve to help those under persecution understand that the suffering they were undergoing derived from a wrathful Satan unleashed upon earth, and that they would take comfort in knowing that he hath but a short time. Like most mythological passages, there is meaning behind the personifications. For example, Satan, before it became a proper name for the evil one, meant adversary or accuser in Hebrew and this was translated by the Greek, *diabolos* which, before it meant devil meant slanderer. This indicates that those who were attempting to personify the force of an evil will within man, saw this force as the enemy who first tempted man to do wrong, and then, having succeeded, tormented him with accusations of his wrongdoing.

Those of us well acquainted with the agony of guilt and the healing of forgiveness experience something which gives this kind of personification of evil great meaning. However, as if suggested above, the significance of the passage is most important in worship, rather than in its literal meaning. The feast of St.

Michael and All Angels exists in our calendar because it attests to a reality which we can only understand in mythological and mystical terms, and through this epistle we can draw hope and strength from the assurance of the eventual triumph of good over evil without literal knowledge of how it will take place. We apprehend in worship what we cannot grasp in discourse, and it is here that the greatest value of the Revelation lies.

An even more important example is in the epistle for the first Sunday after Pentecost, or Trinity Sunday, in the C Year in the Proposed Book of Common Prayer which is the very beginning of John's vision of heaven.

After this I looked, and there before my eyes was a door opened in heaven; and the voice that I had first heard speaking to me like a trumpet said, 'Come up here, and I will show you what must happen hereafter.' At once I was caught up by the Spirit. There in heaven stood a throne, and on the throne sat one whose appearance was like the gleam of jasper and cornelian; and round the throne was a rainbow, bright as an emerald. In a circle about this throne were twenty-four other thrones, and on them sat twenty-four elders, robed in white and wearing crowns of gold. From the throne went out flashes of lightning and peals of thunder. Burning before the throne were seven flaming torches, the seven spirits of God, and in front of it stretched what seemed a sea of glass, like a sheet of ice.

In the centre, round the throne itself, were four living creatures, covered with eyes, in front and behind. The first creature was like a lion, the second like an ox, the third had a human face, the fourth was like an eagle in flight. The four living creatures, each of them with six wings, had eyes all over, inside and out; and by day and by night without a pause they sang:

'Holy, holy, holy is God the sovereign Lord of all, who was, and is, and is to come!'

As often as the living creatures give glory and honour and thanks to the One who sits on the throne, who lives for ever and ever, the twenty-four elders fall down before the One who sits on the throne and worship him who lives for ever and ever; and as they lay their crowns before the throne they cry:

'Thou art worthy, O Lord our God, to receive glory and honour and power, because thou didst create all things; by thy will they were created, and have their being!'

(Rev. 4:1-11 NEB)

Of course, we can make all sorts of references to the origin of the images used, for example, the combination of Isaiah 6 and Ezekiel 1 for the living creatures. We can talk about the parallels in Babylonian mythology, or identify the four and twenty elders with the patriarchs of the twelve tribes and the twelve apostles, and we might speculate on references to the zodiac or see in the living creatures the four evangelists. But if we do all these things, what have we done? We have enmeshed ourselves in trivia and have missed the point of the passage. We need to be caught in the glory and splendor of the scene, to sing the thrice Holy with the creatures, to cast down whatever crowns we may have before the throne with the elders and to chant the "Holy, Holy, Holy" with them and ponder the meaning of the great and mysterious truth for ourselves in the final verse:

For thou hast created all things, and for thy pleasure they were and are created.

Perhaps not as full of power, majesty and glory as the Trinity epistle, but to me more touchingly beautiful in a more human way is the epistle for All Saints' Day. It is on this day that we honor those Saints who are known only to God and those humans whose lives they touched. This is a very personal kind of celebration, for each worshiper carries love and thanksgiving in his heart for those dear ones who, by living close to God, received their streaks of light which they passed on to him. I can see those close to me in the scene described below.

After this I looked and saw a vast throng, which no one could count, from every nation, of all tribes, peoples, and languages, standing in front of the throne and before the Lamb. They were robed in white and had palms in their hands, and they shouted together:

'Victory to our God who sits on the throne, and to the Lamb!'

And all the angels stood around the throne and the elders and the four living creatures, and they fell on their faces before the throne and worshipped God, crying:

'Amen! Praise and glory and wisdom, thanksgiving and honour, power and might, be to our God for ever and ever! Amen.'

Then one of the elders turned to me and said, 'These men that are robed in white—who are they and from where do they come?' But I answered, 'My lord, you know, not I.' Then he said to me, 'These are the men who have passed through the great ordeal; they have washed their robes and made them white in the blood of the Lamb. That is why they stand before the throne of God and minister to him day and night in his temple; and he who sits on the throne will dwell with them. They shall never again feel hunger or thirst, the sun shall not beat on them nor any scorching heat, because the Lamb who is at the heart of the throne will be their shepherd and will guide them to the springs of the water of life; and God will wipe all tears from their eyes.'

(Rev. 7:9-17 NEB)

One can no more comment on this passage than explain why a song is beautiful, or a joke is funny, or why it is you love someone. Either you bring to it an experience of the Saints of God which illuminates it for you, or it is nonsense. Many people identify saints with religion, church, piety or even hypocrisy, and in so doing, don't recognize God's saints when they meet them. When these saints are recognized in your life for what they are, this epistle will come to life for you.

This chapter promised a glimpse into heaven and that is what Saint John the Divine is trying to give us. However, we must bring to his work a longing for God and a desire for heaven. It is the Spirit of God in John that speaks to the Spirit of God in us and communicates His meaning to us. It is not the kind of communication that speaks solely, or even principally, to the mind, but to the heart and soul. The Revelation is an attempt to transcend a barrier beyond knowledge and reason where neither senses nor logic can go. Yet we can transcend that barrier, in the Spirit, as John says it. The fact that this Revelation, which did not surely meet the criteria set up for inclusion in the New Testament, is included in it is testimony to its capacity to transmit the authenticity of the Spirit to our spirit and bring us into communication with God.

Discussion Guide

How can we discuss heaven? We can anticipate it, savor it, contemplate it, enjoy our glimpse of it, but there is little to discuss. So I am leaving a passage with you for that purpose. Think about the questions I raise if you like, but more important, savor and enjoy.

Then I saw a new heaven and a new earth, for the first heaven and the first earth had vanished, and there was no longer any sea. I saw the holy city, new Jerusalem, coming down out of heaven from God, made ready like a bride adorned for her husband. I heard a loud voice proclaiming from the throne: 'Now at last God has his dwelling among men! He will dwell among them and they shall be his people, and God himself will be with them. He will wipe every tear from their eyes; and there shall be an end to death, and to mourning and crying and pain; for the old order has passed away!'

Then he who sat on the throne said, 'Behold, I am making all things new!' (And he said to me, 'Write this down; for these words are trustworthy and true. Indeed, they are already fulfilled.') 'I am Alpha and Omega, the beginning and the end. A draught from the water-springs of life will be my free gift to the thirsty. All this is the victor's heritage; and I will be his God and he shall be my son.'

(Rev. 21:1-7 NEB)

The vision of the New Jerusalem permeates the whole Bible—we find implicit in the Fall, explicit throughout the book. Concurrently we encounter the theme of the bride, the new Israel, coming down without spot or wrinkle, adorned for her husband. Here they meet. What now happens to the streaks of light? What is the implication for them in the phrase, "God has his dwelling among men"? What does the passing of the old order mean to you?

The first paragraph is John's description of what he sees happening. The second is God's proclamation of its meaning. What differences do you notice?

Afterword

Throughout this book we have met the Holy Spirit in passing without much comment, not because we are not aware of His indispensable role but because we are saving the best until last.

Jesus prepares His disciples for His eventual parting from them by promising, on numerous occasions that He will send the Holy Spirit to be with them when He leaves. Here is one of the most explicit of these:

'If you love me you will obey my commands; and I will ask the Father, and he will give you another to be your Advocate, who will be with you for ever—the Spirit of truth. The world . . . neither sees nor knows him; but you know him, because he dwells with you and is in you. I will not leave you bereft; I am coming back to you. In a little while the world will see me no longer, but you will see me; because I live, you too will live; then you will know that I am in my Father, and you in me and I in you. The man who has received my commands and obeys them—he it is who loves me; and he who loves me will be loved by my Father; and I will love him and disclose myself to him.'

Judas asked him—the other Judas, not Iscariot—'Lord, what can have happened, that you mean to

disclose yourself to us alone and not to the world?' Jesus replied, 'Anyone who loves me will heed what I say; then my Father will love him, and we will come to him and make our dwelling with him; but he who does not love me does not heed what I say. And the word you hear is not mine; it is the word of the Father who sent me. I have told you all this while I am still here with you; but your Advocate, the Holy Spirit whom the Father will send in my name, will teach you everything, and will call to mind all that I have told you.
(John 14:15-26 NEB)

In this version the Greek title, *Paraclete* is translated advocate. This imparts some of the meaning of the original but we have no one word which translates all of it, an advocate, literally, "Speaks to you" giving you helpful advice, telling you the truth. But there is an idea of forceful communication by the Holy Spirit in the word Paraclete. The King James Version gets this idea with the title comforter if we use the original meaning as one who comes *Cum Fortis*, "with strength." I vacillate between convincer and persuader when I translate the word. It is clear then that the Holy Spirit comes to us to lead us into all truth with powerful persuasion. He is the Spirit of truth itself. We begin to perceive through this promise of Jesus to send Him that He must have been the source of the streaks of light all along. But He is much more, Jesus promises over and over to send Him to the disciples. Let us see how He keeps His promise,

Late that Sunday evening, when the disciples were together behind locked doors, for fear of the Jews, Jesus came and stood among them. 'Peace be with you!' he said, and then showed them his hands and his side. So when the disciples saw the

Lord, they were filled with joy. Jesus repeated, 'Peace be with you!', and said, 'As the Father sent me, so I send you.' Then he breathed on them, saying, 'Receive the Holy Spirit!'

(John 20:19-22 NEB)

And so the disciples received the Holy Spirit as promised, but this is not all. John the Baptist talks about Jesus coming to baptize with the Holy Spirit. Jesus himself admonishes the disciples to go to Jerusalem and wait.

While he was in their company he told them not to leave Jerusalem. 'You must wait', he said, 'for the promise made by my Father, about which you have heard me speak: John, as you know, baptized with water, but you will be baptized with the Holy Spirit, and within the next few days.'

(Acts 1:4-5 NEB)

'But you will receive power when the Holy Spirit comes upon you; and you will bear witness for me in Jerusalem and all over Judaea and Samaria, and away to the ends of the earth.'

(Acts 1:8 NEB)

Jesus had already given the Holy Spirit to the disciples when He breathed on them, just as the Holy Spirit is given to us in our baptism with water. Everyone baptized as a Christian receives all of the Holy Spirit there is to give—*potentially*. So also even to the apostles the Holy Spirit was given in *potential* the authority to accept, bind and loose, all that was given at that time. It remained for the power of the Spirit to be given in the baptism of the Holy Spirit. Baptism is used in many senses in the Greek language but they seem to boil down to the pouring out of something upon someone which changes them. Water is poured on us so that we who were dirty become clean. The pouring out of the Holy Spirit upon us releases the Spirit dwelling in us from its *potential* state into its *actual* state. We are baptized of the Holy Spirit so that the power bestowed upon us may be released. The gifts of the Spirit vary as the twelfth chapter of 1 Corinthians makes quite clear. The Spirit is manifested in us by the gift of power hitherto unused by us. It may come as a response to our prayer, the prayer of others, or an inner call. Power is given as it is required. Many people associate the gift of speaking in tongues as a necessary manifestation of the baptism of the Holy Spirit. Although this gift has been given to me in one of the most powerful experiences of my life, I believe I was Spirit-filled long before this gift was given, I felt, literally felt, anointment by the Spirit when God called me to the priesthood.

All this is to show that streaks of light are given by the Holy Spirit and open us to other gifts. The Bible is a way to God, a way to make the acquaintance of the Holy Spirit. This is why I have written this book. The Holy Spirit dwells in us so that we can *actualize* what is given us in *potential*. He is there always, as close as breath, to lead us into all truth. He supplies us with many more streaks of light, than we perceive. He is there constantly, striving against our blindness.

What a difference it makes as we become increasingly sensitive to Him. We perceive the transmission more frequently and with much more illumination. The first hurdle to overcome is faith that He is there faithfully transmitting. We can expect Him. We can count on Him, when we approach the Bible with this attitude we make a good beginning. But there is much more.

I frequently asked you in the discussion guides to read between the lines, rather than parrot what the text says. Your creativity, your lively imagination is the instrument upon which the Spirit plays. If it is locked in the case, not much music is going to be made. Don't try to tell me you don't possess such an instrument. God gave one to each of us, all of them unique in their individual contribution to the heavenly harmonies. It is from this that the understanding springs, for in offering ourselves to the Spirit we receive bountifully from Him.

Learning to meditate on a small portion of Scripture each day opens us increasingly to the Spirit. I have done this with varying degrees of faithfulness for twenty-five years. I can only marvel at where I might be now if I had been constantly faithful. But how can I tell you how to meditate?

> Three things there are which are too
>   wonderful for me,
>   four which I do not understand:
>   the way of a vulture in the sky,
>   the way of a serpent on the rock,
>   the way of a ship out at sea,
>   and the way of man with a girl.
>   (Prov. 30:18-19 NEB)

I would add a fifth. The way of the Holy Spirit with man.

I begin to teach people to meditate by asking them to:

1) Name the passage they have chosen for meditation (three to five words).
2) Tell what God is saying to you in the passage.
3) Tell your objections, why you don't want to obey.
4) Resolve the conflict.

I began this way, carefully writing everything down. I guess it served the purpose of starting me. But I got so bored with that method I couldn't use it consistently even in the discussion guides for this book. Incidently, the passages and questions in the discussion guide might get you started. But the instrument is yours and you will eventually learn to play your own music.

But the streaks of light are just the beginning. We spoke of the lay apostolate some time back. The streaks of light help you to be an apostle and being stimulates doing and doing develops new levels of being. If this book has helped you find your apostolate it has fulfilled its purpose.

One last frightening thing. Think big—Jesus' life shows you what your life is meant to be. You, as He promises, can do all that He did. Certainly His words tell it best.

> Believe me when I say that I am in the Father and the Father in me; or else accept the evidence of the deeds themselves. In truth, in very truth I tell you, he who has faith in me will do what I am doing; and he will do greater things still because I am going to the Father.
>
> (John 14:11-12 NEB)